John Thomson

The Life of Faith

as Illustrated by the example of the Apostle Paul - with brief notice of one of the

grounds of faith

John Thomson

The Life of Faith
as Illustrated by the example of the Apostle Paul - with brief notice of one of the grounds of faith

ISBN/EAN: 9783337332518

Printed in Europe, USA, Canada, Australia, Japan

Cover: Foto ©Lupo / pixelio.de

More available books at **www.hansebooks.com**

THE LIFE OF FAITH

AS ILLUSTRATED BY THE EXAMPLE OF

THE APOSTLE PAUL.

WITH

A BRIEF NOTICE

OF ONE OF

THE GROUNDS OF FAITH.

BY

JOHN THOMSON, D.D.,

PAISLEY,

AUTHOR OF "THE DOMESTIC CIRCLE."

"The just shall live by his faith."—HAB. ii. 4.

EDINBURGH:
JOHNSTONE, HUNTER, & CO.
LONDON: HAMILTON, ADAMS, & CO.
1876.

EDINBURGH:
PRINTED BY M'FARLANE AND ERSKINE,
ST JAMES SQUARE.

PREFATORY NOTE.

WHILE the title of this volume expresses with perhaps sufficient clearness the object which the Author had in view in preparing it, yet it may be desirable to explain that it is specially designed for the young, and more particularly for that important and interesting class of them who form the rising hope of the country and of the Church—viz., our Young Men. The subjects treated of were employed by the Author in a winter course of instruction to the young men of his own congregation; and the interest awakened in them encouraged the hope that they might prove useful in a wider sphere. Accordingly the substance of them appeared in a series of articles which were published in that excellent periodical *The Christian Treasury;* and at the suggestion of several brethren, they are now presented to the public in this more permanent form, the preparation of which has been a source of great pleasure to the Author during a period of rest and relaxation from active duty. And though the volume makes no pretensions to originality, yet he trusts that if accompanied by the needed blessing, it may not be uninteresting or unprofitable to those for whom it is specially designed.

It may also be stated that the leading thought

which is intended to run through the volume is that expressed by the prophet, and frequently referred to by the apostle Paul, "The just shall live by his faith." It is important to show our young men that they cannot either begin to live, or continue to live to God, without faith in Him who is both the Author and Sustainer of the new life in the soul; but that having this faith abiding in them and constantly exercised, the new life becomes a necessity, as well as a source of peace and strength and hope.

It will also be observed that the life of Paul, exhibited in his writings and actings, is specially referred to, and presented as a model to the young. His many-sided character is analysed, and the various graces with which it was so remarkably adorned are set forth in combination, in order to show that in him faith produced not only a great but a well-balanced mind, a symmetrical character, and a consistent life.

In the supplementary part of the volume on the "Grounds of Faith," a specimen is given of one of the branches of Christian evidence, which may not be without use in this age of unsettled opinion and prejudiced doubt, and which may tend to lead our young men to study those other branches of the Christian evidence that demonstrate that the Bible is no cunningly devised fable, but the inspired Word of God. The substance of this part of the volume formed a series of articles in the *Christian Evidence Journal*, which has rendered such good service to the cause of Apologetics.

CONTENTS.

The Life of Faith.

CHAPTER I.

	PAGE
INTRODUCTION,	1
1. Christian Fidelity,	4
2. Christian Patience,	7
3. Personal Piety,	11

CHAPTER II.

THE COMBINATION OF GRACES,	16
1. Christian Humility,	18
2. Moral Dignity,	27

CHAPTER III.

1. LARGE-HEARTEDNESS,	33
(1.) In a noble aim,	36
(2.) In an ardent pursuit of it,	39
(3.) In forgiveness of injuries,	44
2. TENDER-HEARTEDNESS,	47
(1.) In tears of suffering,	49
(2.) In tears of sympathy,	50
(3.) In tears of solicitude for others,	50

CHAPTER IV.

1. UNSELFISHNESS,	54
(1.) In renouncing worldly prospects,	57
(2.) In refusing worldly advantages,	59
(3.) In seeking the good of others,	66

2. CONSCIENTIOUSNESS, ... 68
   (1.) Honesty in money matters, ... 70
   (2.) Fidelity to the Master, ... 72

CHAPTER V.

1. CHRISTIAN COURAGE, ... 74
   (1.) In resisting enemies, ... 78
   (2.) In opposing friends, ... 79
   (3.) Qualifications of a good soldier of Christ, . 84
2. HABITUAL PRAYERFULNESS, ... 87

CHAPTER VI.

GROWTH IN GRACE, ... 94
   Sunset of life, ... 97
   Fruit in old age, ... 99

CHAPTER VII.

THE NEAR PROSPECT OF DEATH, ... 110
   Hope in death, ... 113
   Support in affliction, ... 115
   Faithful to the end, ... 118
   Crossing the Jordan, ... 122
   Victory over death, ... 125

CHAPTER VIII.

INNER SOURCE OF THE LIFE OF FAITH, . . . 131
   1. Life from Christ, ... 138
   2. Life by Christ, ... 140
   3. Life for Christ, ... 142
   4. The power of faith, ... 145
      (1.) Faith gives new meaning to life, . . 146
      (2.) Faith supplies a new motive, . . . 148
      (3.) Faith imparts new strength, . . . 150

Contents. vii

CHAPTER IX.

	PAGE
FAITH IN ITS PRACTICAL RESULTS,	153
1. Steadfastness of faith,	156
2. Immovableness of hope,	159
3. Active service,	161
4. Motives to it,	166

Grounds of Faith.

THE QUESTION AS TO THE REALITY OF MIRACLES STATED,	175
CHAP. I.—The Possibility of a Miracle,	178
,, II.—The Probability of Miracles,	180
,, III.—Value of Miracles as Evidences,	182
,, IV.—How Miracles can prove Doctrines,	184
,, V.—Infidel objections refuted,	188
,, VI.—Illustration of the Argument,	199
The reality of the Miracles of Moses shown—	
1. From his personal character,	201
2. From the acknowledgment by the nation at the time,	203
3. From the impossibility of obtaining the nation's belief in the miracles in any subsequent age, unless they were real,	206

" 'Live while ye live,' the sensualist may say,
And catch the pleasures of the passing day.
'Live while ye live,' the holy man replies,
And give to God each moment as it flies.
Lord, in my life let both united be,
I live in pleasure, when I live to Thee."
—COWPER.

THE LIFE OF FAITH.

CHAPTER I.

INTRODUCTION.

"Not I, but the grace of God which was with me."
—1 COR. xv. 10.

THE Bible is, to a certain extent, a book of biographies. It contains not only the doctrines of a divine creed, and the precepts of a divine law, but also numerous and graphic narratives of the sayings and doings of "the excellent of the earth." It teaches us by examples, and shows how its heavenly doctrines have been embodied in personal character, and its holy precepts exemplified in living action. Among these Bible biographies, the only perfect one is, of course, the life of Christ, as portrayed by the four Evangelists. In their simple and truthful narratives we have, as it were, four distinct photographic views of Him, who was "fairer than the children of men," and of whom the infidel Rousseau declared, in an involuntary burst of admiration, "that the inventor of such a character would be more wonderful than the hero."

But while Christ himself is the only perfect pattern of moral excellence, yet we may learn much from a careful study of the biographies of eminent saints, with which Scripture abounds. Though our chief aim must be to follow Christ, in that spotless example which He has left for our imitation, yet we ought also to be "followers of those who, through faith and patience, inherit the promises;" and though their failings and mistakes should be beacons of warning to us, yet the graces which adorned their character, and the virtues which ennobled their lives, should stimulate and encourage us to exemplify, in our own conduct, the power of a living Christianity.

It will readily be admitted that, in that bright "cloud of witnesses" with which we are compassed about, none stands forth more conspicuous and illustrious than the great Apostle of the Gentiles; and that, in his many-sided character, none can be more advantageously held forth as a model for young men. Most truly could Paul say that he had laboured in the cause of Christ "more abundantly" than any of his fellow-apostles. And yet for these abundant labours, as well as for his distinguished attainments, he never imagined that any merit or credit was due to himself. On the contrary, he accounted himself "the least of the apostles," yea, "less than the least of all saints." He felt deeply that nothing which he did was, strictly speaking, his own doing, but rather the doing of the Lord by his feeble instrumentality. In his outward aspect there was nothing to command attention or to enforce submission, for his enemies said of him that his "bodily presence was weak, and his speech contemptible." And though this, in their lips, may have been the language of exaggeration, yet, probably, he had a weakly frame and an ungainly address, which nothing could have overcome but the force of his intellect, and the fervour of his spirit, and, above all, the omnipotent grace of God. And yet this man, with his sickly body but courageous soul, with his thorn in the flesh—the messenger of Satan—to buffet him, but with the grace of God made sufficient for him; this man achieved the noblest triumphs over pagan idolatry and vice, and planted the standard of the Cross in the chief centres of power, throughout the vast Roman empire, and was the main instrument in accomplishing a moral revolution, such as the world has never seen before nor since. The other apostles, indeed, were not idle; but of the great Apostle of the Gentiles it may be truly said, "Many have done virtuously, but thou excellest them all." And need we be told that the same grace which made him what he was, can make us like him; and that the heights of piety, and virtue, and usefulness, to which he rose, are not inaccessible to us; for "with God is the residue of the Spirit."

We purpose, therefore, to analyse the character of the apostle Paul, and to exhibit it as an example of living Christianity, or the life of faith, and especially as a model for young men. They are the rising hope of our country and of the Church. Many of them have shared richly in the blessings of a time of revival, and have resolved to devote themselves to the work to which Paul's whole life was consecrated; and it may be useful to them to fix their attention on his character and labours, and to learn from them those lessons of wisdom which they are fitted and designed to teach; and it may be useful to others, by inducing them to devote their energies to the cause of Christ, and to the extension of His kingdom in the world.

In this introductory chapter we shall endeavour to present merely a general view of Paul's character in three leading aspects; and in subsequent chapters we shall enter more into detail, and exhibit, specifically, the more prominent features of his character.

I. His Faithfulness as a Preacher of Christ.

There are many, in the present day, who undervalue, and even despise, the preaching of the Gospel and who regard it as foolish and fanatical to expect that the words, spoken by a fellow-mortal from the pulpit, will reform men's lives, and renovate their hearts. But they forget that the preaching of the Gospel is an ordinance of Christ; and that, however feeble or defective the instrument in itself may be, yet it becomes "mighty through God." Whenever His Word is preached simply, faithfully, and earnestly, it will not return to Him void: and "it hath pleased God, by the foolishness of preaching, to save them that believe."

But while this notion is entertained by the sceptical, it is strange that a similar notion is entertained also by the superstitious. For instance, the Romanist and the Ritualist undervalue public preaching, and attach far greater importance to baptism and other external rites. But that was not the opinion of the apostle Paul; for he says, " Christ sent me, not to baptize, but to preach the Gospel," plainly intimating that no outward observances can for a moment be put in comparison with a full and faithful proclamation of the Gospel. It was for this end mainly that he was converted to the faith of Christ, and it was to this that he consecrated all the energies of his gifted mind, and all the activities of his busy life. "Necessity is laid upon me," he said, "yea, woe is unto me, if I preach not the Gospel." In this he was never idle, but he went from house to house, from city to city, and from one country to another, preaching, in season and out of season, the glad tidings which were proclaimed on the plains of Bethlehem by the angelic host, "Unto you is born a Saviour, who is Christ the Lord." Accordingly, we find that the whole substance of his preaching is summed up in such words as these: "I determined not to know anything among you save Jesus Christ and Him crucified;" "I am not ashamed of the Gospel of Christ;" "God forbid that I should glory, save in the cross of our Lord Jesus Christ."

From all this, it is clear that, as a herald of salvation, his trumpet gave no uncertain sound, and that he left no one in doubt as to the meaning of the message which he brought. His teaching was uniformly clear and definite, simple and decided. Everywhere he proclaimed ruin by sin, and redemption by grace; the guilt of the sinner and the glory of the Saviour; the depravity of the human heart, and the sanctifying power of the Spirit; the helplessness of man and the sovereign grace of God; the inefficacy of good works to justify us, and yet the absolute necessity of good works to prove that we have been justified. These are some of the leading topics which formed the essence of Paul's preaching, and on which he never ceased to enlarge with glowing fervour. And these vital truths are the only lever power by which man can be lifted up out of the depths of his guilt, and misery, and moral degradation, and restored to the favour and image of God, and made meet for the inheritance of the saints in light. It is not by moral essays, or misty statements, or ritual observances, that man can be extricated from the horrible pit, and set upon the Rock; but it is only by the simple story of the Cross, by the truth as it is in Jesus, preached with apostolic fervour, and impressed upon the heart by Divine grace. And the more closely the preaching of modern times comes to resemble the preaching of Paul in its simplicity and faithfulness, in its directness and fervour, in its lucid statements of doctrine, and in its warm appeals to the conscience and the heart, the more confidently may we expect similar results in the conversion of sinners, and the consecration of saints to the service of Christ. Let young men, then, prize the simple Gospel, and seek to profit by the preaching of it. Let them beware of itching ears, and a craving after novelty and mere excitement; and, "as new-born babes, let them desire the sincere milk of the Word, that they may grow thereby."

II. His Patience as a Sufferer for Christ.

"I will show him" (said Christ to Ananias at Damascus) "how great things he must *suffer* for my name's sake;" as if one main purpose for which he was converted had been to endure suffering. These sufferings began as soon as he was known to be a Christian. Then he "suffered the loss of all things" for Christ. He forfeited the good opinion of his former friends, and the high esteem in which he was held by his Jewish brethren, and all his dazzling prospects of worldly advancement. But what things were gain to him, these he counted loss for Christ; and he willingly parted with all, in order that he might "win Christ, and be found in Him." No sooner did he open his mouth at Damascus to preach Christ in the synagogues, than "the Jews watched the gates day and night to kill him." And all through the thirty-two years of his public ministry, he met with similar treatment both from Jews and Gentiles. At Lystra, he was nearly stoned to death. At Philippi, he was scourged with rods, and cast into prison, and fettered in the stocks. At Thessalonica, the mob assaulted the house of Jason where he lodged, and compelled him to flee for his life. At Corinth, he was dragged before the judgment-seat of Gallio, but for whose protection he would have been subjected to indignity and cruelty. At Ephesus, the whole city was thrown into an uproar, raised by the silversmiths; and if the mob could have seized him, they would have torn him to pieces. At Jerusalem, the rulers plotted against him, and the people beat him in the very temple, and went about to kill him. These, however, were but a few of his sufferings, and many have been left unrecorded, except incidentally in his own epistles. It was literally true that in every city bonds and afflictions awaited him. Read the affecting account which he gives of his sufferings, not in the language of boasting, but in self-defence against those false teachers, who sought to weaken his authority, and to mar his usefulness—2 Cor. xi. 23, 25: "Are they ministers of Christ? (I speak as a fool), I am more: in labours more abundant, in stripes above measure, in prisons more frequent, in deaths oft. Thrice was I beaten with rods, once was I stoned, thrice I suffered shipwreck, a night and a day I have been in the deep." These words were written about twelve years before his martyrdom; and we might have expected that his lofty heroism and warm benevolence would thenceforth turn aside the hatred and hostility even of his bitterest enemies. But no; for, even to the last, he was subjected to great sorrow and suffering, and was the object of relentless persecution. The world hated, and hunted to death, one of its greatest benefactors, and requited his love with ever deepening malignity and cruelty, till at length it robbed him of his life, and sent him *home* to obtain the martyr's crown.

But, amid all these protracted and intense sufferings, the apostle possessed his soul in patience. They did not sour his spirit, nor quench his zeal, nor dry up the gushing fountains of his love to man. The more bitterly they hated him, the more actively did he labour, and the more fervently did he pray, for their salvation. Here truly was "another spirit" from that which is natural to man. Mere flesh and blood would have shrunk back from such sufferings. In such a sea of trouble foaming around him, any man, if unaided by heavenly grace, would have been engulfed. Manifestly, it was the power of Christ resting upon him, and the love of Christ constraining him, and the hope of glory inspiring him, that enabled the apostle to endure such trials, not only with calm tranquillity, but even with exulting triumph. "We glory," he says, "in tribulations also, knowing that tribulation worketh patience, and patience experience, and experience hope; and hope maketh not ashamed, because the love of God is shed abroad in our hearts by the Holy Ghost, which is given unto us." Thus, patience in him had its perfect work; for he could bear his trials without murmuring, and perform his duties without discouragement, and wait for the promised blessings without despondency.

Here then is a pattern for the imitation of young men. If they are faithful to Christ, they must lay their account with self-denial, and suffering, and the world's hatred. If indeed they are content to walk according to the course of this world, they will escape that hostility, which is the lot of all who will live godly in Christ Jesus. But surely it is better to suffer than to sin; better to endure the world's hatred than God's displeasure; better to regulate our conduct by strict Christian principle than to be driven hither and thither by every wind that blows, amid the ever-shifting currents of human opinion. By conforming to the world, in its pleasures and maxims, in its aims and spirit, we may gain its favour and applause; but what will that profit us, if in so doing we displease God? We cannot both be lovers of pleasure and lovers of God. The combination is impossible, and the compromise is vain. When Christ calls us to follow Him, He plainly tells us that we must deny ourselves, and take up our cross daily. But then He makes the burden light to those who trust in His promised grace; and He tells us too, that the cross will soon be exchanged for the crown, and the sword of conflict for the palm of victory.

III. His Piety as a Genuine Disciple of Christ.

This was the true secret of Paul's success as a preacher of Christ, and of his patience as a sufferer for Christ. His activity in labouring, and his patience in enduring, proceeded from his personal experience of an inward work of grace, without which his labours would soon have ceased, and his trials would have overwhelmed him. It is said of the insincere man, "Will he always call upon God?" No! for his interest in spiritual things will decay, and his love will wax cold, and his zeal will evaporate, like the morning cloud when chased by the hurricane. But on the other hand, "the righteous shall hold on his way, and he that hath clean hands shall wax stronger and stronger."

Such was the apostle Paul; and all that he wrote, and did, shows that he was a deeply exercised Christian. In reading his epistles, we can read his inmost soul, and we can see that his religion was deeply rooted there, and that all the fair blossoms and rich fruit which his outer life exhibited grew out necessarily from the *inner life* that he had derived from his personal union to Christ. He knew full well that a man might preach eloquently to others, and yet be himself a castaway; and therefore he was careful to keep his body in subjection, and to mortify the flesh with all its affections and lusts. He knew that a man might have eminent gifts, splendid talents, and a fair outward profession, and yet be destitute of saving grace, and a stranger to the power of godliness; and therefore, in watching for the souls of others, he did not forget to watch for his own soul with scrupulous care, lest Satan should gain an advantage over him, and lest sin should resume its former ascendency over him. He knew that a man might point out to others the way to heaven, like a finger-post fixed on the roadside, while, like it, he never moves one step himself in that direction; and therefore he continually exercised himself to maintain "a conscience void of offence toward God and man," that so, with an unencumbered step, and an unburdened conscience, he might go on, from strength to strength, in the way to Zion.

Personal Piety. 13

Those who know what Christian experience is, cannot fail to trace unmistakable evidence in Paul's epistles, that he was a deeply exercised Christian, and that the gushing streams of warm affection and generous action, which appeared in his outer life, welled forth from a living fountain within. Not only does he describe the experience of other Christians, but he describes his own, in language of great simplicity, but of deepest pathos and singular power. He knew what it was to be pressed down under the burden of conscious guilt and the load of indwelling sin. He knew what it was to realise and feel the inward conflict, between grace and nature, between the Spirit and the flesh, between the new man and the old. And he knew what it was to come as the chief of sinners to the loving Saviour, and to trust in His atoning blood for pardon, and to rely on His promised grace for sanctification. And then, how touchingly does he speak of his *faith* in the mercy of God and in the merits of Christ; and of his *gratitude* for the blessings of salvation; and of his *love* to Him who gave Himself for us; and of his intense desire for deliverance from sin, and for perfect conformity to God's will; and of his ever brightening hope of the coming glory. And yet, with all that bright array of Christian graces which adorned his character, how deep was his humility, how dissatisfied was he with all that he had yet attained, and how earnestly did he press forward to higher attainments and holier services. "Not" (he says) "as though I had already attained, either were already perfect; but forgetting those things which are behind, and reaching forth unto those things which are before, I press toward the mark, for the prize of the high calling of God in Christ Jesus."

Let all then, and especially let the young, seek to imitate Paul in his deep Christian experience. Though few can hope to emulate him, either as a powerful preacher, or as a patient sufferer, yet all may, and all must, imitate him as a devoted and deeply exercised Christian, otherwise their hopes of heaven can never be realised. Let us, like Paul, seek to have a quickened conscience, a simple faith in Christ, a sincere love to Him, and an earnest determination to walk in His holy footsteps. Let us always be on our guard against the evil that is within us, as well as against the temptations that are without. And while cherishing a growing sense of imperfection and shortcoming, let us also cherish a growing desire for clearer light, for warmer love, and more devoted obedience. And whatever attainments we may make in the divine life, and whatever services we may render to Christ, let us ever say, in all lowliness and meekness, "Not I, but the grace of God which was with me."

In the next chapter we shall endeavour to analyse the character of the apostle, and to point out in detail some of its leading features, and their remarkable combination. More especially we shall speak of these two, viz., his deep humility, combined with high moral dignity.

CHAPTER II.

THE COMBINATION OF GRACES.

"Unto me, who am less than the least of all saints, is this grace given, that I should preach among the Gentiles the unsearchable riches of Christ."—EPH. iii. 8.

HAVING already presented, in the former chapter, a general outline of the character of Paul, as a preacher, as a sufferer, and as a true believer, we come now to analyse his character more minutely, and to exhibit its more prominent features in detail. Many of these features have been often and fully described by able and eloquent writers, such as the late Dr M'Crie and the Rev. Adolph Monod, whose keen sagacity and power of discrimination cannot be surpassed by any attempt to treat of the same subject, and who have furnished ample and valuable materials, for attaining a clear and just perception of the many-sided character of the great apostle. But while taking advantage of these materials, we propose to adopt a somewhat different method. Instead of considering the qualities of Paul's gifted mind singly and separately, we propose to consider them *in combination*, with the view of showing how apparently opposite qualities were harmonised in his wonderful character, so as to produce, as the result, not only a great, but a thoroughly well-balanced mind. There have often been great and good men, who were distinguished by one or more remarkable excellences; but whose moral power was weakened or destroyed by glaring defects, which were only rendered more conspicuous in the light of their acknowledged excellences. Superior genius, as in Lord Byron, has often been allied with a low morality. High intellectual power has often been combined with what is disreputable and base. And even true piety and strict integrity have often been combined with want of judgment and flagrant folly. Of the distinguished founder of the inductive philosophy, Lord Bacon, it has been truly said, that while he was the greatest and wisest, he was also "the meanest of mankind."

But no such want of symmetry or harmony can be detected in the character of Paul. While he was possessed of the noblest qualities, in the highest state of development, yet they are all of a piece, beautifully blended, and harmoniously adjusted, so as to give the impression of singular power and commanding influence. In this respect, therefore, the apostle's character is an almost perfect model for young men: and it well deserves their attentive study and close imitation. Even on the mere surface of his character, the most cursory reader can scarcely fail to observe a singular combination, of the highest argumentative power with the most stirring and thrilling eloquence, of the most intrepid courage with the most winning tenderness, of the strongest resolution with meekness and gentleness, and of burning zeal and enthusiasm with profound wisdom and rare sagacity;—all showing that he shines as a star of the first magnitude in the Church's firmament; while, at the same time, he humbly acknowledged that he shone by a borrowed light, for which he was wholly indebted to the glorious Sun of Righteousness.

Following out, then, the plan now indicated, of presenting the leading characteristics of Paul in combination, we select the two following, viz.: *His deep humility combined with high moral dignity.*

I. CHRISTIAN HUMILITY.—"Unto me" (he said), "who am less than the least of all saints, is this grace given."

The importance of this grace as an essential element of Christian character, can scarcely be over-estimated. As man fell by pride, so he can only rise again by humility. Pride goes before destruction; but before honour is humility; or as our Lord himself has strongly and tersely expressed it, "He that exalteth himself shall be abased; but he that hum-

Christian Humility.

bleth himself shall be exalted." And we are plainly told that there is no admission into Christ's kingdom, except for those who are made in some degree "meek and lowly in heart," as Christ himself was; "for except ye be converted, and become as little children, ye shall in no wise enter into the kingdom of heaven." Our very first steps heavenward must be, the entire renunciation of every idea of personal merit, and the cordial acceptance of salvation as the gift of free and sovereign grace; for "God resisteth the proud, but He giveth grace to the humble."

But though man, as a dependent and sinful being, has every reason to clothe himself with humility, yet this grace is not natural to any man. Guilty and polluted though he be, yet how ready is he to be puffed up with pride and self-conceit, and to fancy that he "is rich and increased with goods, and has need of nothing," while in reality he is "wretched, and miserable, and poor, and blind, and naked!" That this is the universal tendency of fallen humanity, is evident from the fact, that no traces of this virtue of humility are to be found in the code of heathen morality. The ancient Romans admired and praised other virtues, but they had not even a word in their language to express this virtue. By their word, *humilitas*, they meant utter baseness and cringing servility. To tell a proud Roman that he ought to be humble (*humilis*) in his own esteem, would have been resented by him as a gross personal insult. Not only, however, among the heathen, but also among the chosen people, true humility was scarcely known and seldom practised. The Pharisees, to whom Paul once belonged, were notorious for their arrogance and self-assumption, for their complacent self-righteousness, and their haughty contempt of other men. The apostle thus expresses the sentiments which he once cherished, and of which he was accustomed to boast, in his former state of ignorance and unbelief: "Circumcised the eighth day, of the stock of Israel, of the tribe of Benjamin, an Hebrew of the Hebrews; as touching the law, a Pharisee; concerning zeal, persecuting the Church; touching the righteousness which is in the law, blameless;" but then he adds, "What things were gain to me, those I counted loss for Christ; yea doubtless, and I count all things but loss for the excellency of the knowledge of Christ Jesus my Lord, for whom I have suffered the loss of all things."

Here, then, was one fruit, and indeed the first fruit of his conversion; even a genuine, unaffected, and profound humility, which was manifested by renouncing his own merits as a ground of hope, and distrusting his own strength as a means of sanctification; and by relying on the Saviour's precious blood alone for pardon, and on His promised grace for purity of heart and devotedness of life. And then

Paul's humility was not an occasional or transient feeling, but it was deeply ingrained in his whole character, and it tinged his whole life; and it grew with his growth in grace. When he wrote the words, "Unto me, the least of all saints, is this *grace given*," he had held the office of an apostle for nearly thirty years. That office he habitually recognised as a *grace*, not merited by himself, but freely granted to him by God: while he felt also that all his eminent qualifications for the office must be ascribed, not to his own wisdom or power, but to the power of Divine grace working mightily in his soul. Sometimes he was compelled in self-defence to recount his manifold labours for Christ; but when he does so, he is careful to add, "Not I, but the grace of God which was with me!" And so also when he is forced to speak of his marvellous success in preaching the Gospel, and the evident and abundant seals of his apostleship, he takes no credit or merit to himself, but his language is, "I have planted, Apollos watered; but God gave the increase. So then neither is he that planteth anything, neither he that watereth; but God that giveth the increase!" And yet more, when he speaks of his sufferings for Christ, which were often severe and almost overwhelming, he plainly intimates that he was not sustained by any power in himself; but he says, "I can do all things *through Christ* strengthening me!" And even when he was compelled to speak of himself in the language of commendation, because his enemies had maligned him, in order to injure through him the cause of his Divine Master, he employs language of this kind with evident reluctance and pain. We have an instance of this in 2 Cor. xii. 11, where, in giving proofs of his apostleship, not only from "the signs and wonders and mighty deeds" which he had wrought, but also from the sufferings which he had endured for Christ, and from the visions and revelations vouchsafed to him, when he was "caught up into paradise," he adds, but "I am become a fool in glorying; ye have compelled me: for I ought to have been commended of *you;* for in nothing am I behind the very chiefest apostles, *though I be nothing.*" This irrepressible burst of wounded feeling reveals the deep-toned humility of his spirit, and the pain and distress which it gave him to be compelled to speak of himself or of his own doings at all. Like a father speaking to his beloved children, he gently reproves his children in the faith for allowing him to be put into such a position, by their neglecting to speak in his defence, and leaving to him the irksome task of self-vindication. But lest, even in doing so, he should be misunderstood, he "begins by acknowledging that he had spoken as a fool, and ends by saying that he was nothing!"

Nor is it difficult to perceive why the apostle was kept so humble, even amid his greatest success. One reason of it was the remembrance of his former enmity to the Saviour, and of the injury he had done to His cause and people. Many were the bitter tears he had shed, and the pangs of self-reproach which he had felt, in reflecting on his former conduct, when he had stifled his convictions, and done many things contrary to the name of Jesus of Nazareth, and breathed out threatenings and slaughter against His disciples; and he could truly say, like the Psalmist, even after his sin was pardoned, "My sin is ever before me." It was this that made him, and kept him, humble in his own estimation. Accordingly, whenever he was compelled to speak of his own attainments or services, he was careful to cast this dark shadow over the brilliancy of his past career; and thus, in writing to the Ephesians, he magnifies that grace of God which was given to him, by calling himself "less than the least of all saints." And in writing to the Corinthians, and referring to his abundant labours, he indulges in the same strain of self-depreciation, saying, "For I am the least of the apostles, that am not meet to be called an apostle, because I persecuted the Church of God!" And just before his martyrdom, in one of the last epistles he ever wrote, he addresses his beloved Timothy in these remarkable words: "I was before a blasphemer, and a persecutor, and injurious: but I obtained mercy, because I did it ignorantly in unbelief. And the grace of our Lord was exceeding abundant with faith and love which is in Christ Jesus. This is a faithful saying, and worthy of all acceptation, that Christ Jesus came into the world to save sinners; of whom I am chief." What a touching exhibition of deep humility is presented in words like these, from the lips of one so highly gifted, and so eminently useful, as the great apostle was. Even at the very close of his laborious life, he confessed that he was "the chief of sinners," and that the only ground of his confidence was that Christ is mighty to save.

But while his humility was deepened by the recollection of his former sins, it was deepened still more by the consciousness of his remaining deficiencies and imperfections. This feeling is very strongly expressed in these well-known words, uttered within a few years of his death—Phil. iii. 12—"Not as though I had already attained, either were already perfect; but I follow after, if that I may apprehend that for which also I am apprehended of Christ Jesus." High as his attainments in Christian excellence unquestionably were, and eminent as his services had been during his laborious life, yet he still felt that he was very far short of perfection, and that everything he did was mixed and marred with sin. Though his character would bear a comparison with that of any other man, yet when he weighed his actions and motives in the balance of the sanctuary, and contrasted them with the perfect example of his Master, he felt and confessed that he needed Divine mercy and grace no less than others. Realising the holiness of Him who cannot tolerate sin, and the strictness of that law which demands a perfect obedience, he felt that he had no ground for boasting, but much cause for humiliation and shame.

Now this painful consciousness of remaining imperfection is one of the surest evidences of living Christianity. Though it may seem paradoxical, yet it is nevertheless true, that the most advanced Christian is always the most humble in his own estimation. And the reason is, not because he is worse than other men, but because he knows his own heart better than other men know theirs; and because he tries himself by a higher and purer standard than they do; and that standard is God's unchangeable law. As he grows in grace, and advances in the divine life, his conscience becomes more tender, and his knowledge of God's law and of his own heart becomes clearer, deeper, and more extensive, so that he discovers sin where he never saw it before. Thus the holier he becomes, the more deeply sensible is he of his remaining defects. As in climbing a hill the prospect becomes more and more extensive; so the higher the Christian ascends in his heavenward path, the wider does the range of his vision become. Thus his past attainments dwindle into insignificance when contrasted with those which he has still to make, just as the hillocks, which looked large when we stood beside them on the plain, seem very small when viewed from the mountain's summit.

Here then is a model for the imitation of young men; and the closer they approach it, the nearer will they come to perfection, the more stable will their character be, the greater their personal influence, and the more extensive their usefulness. If even Paul was humble, much more ought they to be. The remembrance of what they were by nature, and the consciousness of their remaining imperfections, should abase that spirit of pride and self-confidence which is so natural to us all, and should clothe them with that "ornament of a meek and quiet spirit, which in the sight of God is of great price."

Still, however, the consciousness of our deficiencies should not produce either a sluggish feeling of listless indolence, or a morbid feeling of despair. Instead of paralysing the energies of the great apostle, it roused and stimulated him to greater activity, in prosecuting his labours, and in "pressing toward the mark for the prize of his high calling." He did not make his felt imperfections an excuse for resting satisfied with low attainments in Christian excellence; but he rightly judged that, in proportion to the extent of these imperfections, ought to be the measure of his diligence in "reaching forth unto those things which were before." And so must we aim at a high standard of excellence, and aspire after perfect holiness in heart and life. We cannot stand still in the journey to heaven, but we must either advance or recede; and if we are not making progress, we must be losing ground. We are like a man who is rowing a boat against the strong current of a rapid river. If he lie upon his oars, instead of plying them vigorously, then he can make no upward progress, but will be swept helplessly down the stream. All our natural tendencies are downward, and we must resist them, and strive against them, otherwise they will drive us down to the chambers of death.

II. MORAL DIGNITY.

It is not often that humility and dignity are combined, in an equal degree, in the same character. When the former predominates, the character is apt to be soft, timid, and yielding; and when the latter predominates, it is apt to be stern, imperious, and overbearing. But when these two qualities are combined in equal strength, they form a character which is both attractive and venerable, and which awakens both ardent love and profound esteem.

Such, in no ordinary degree, was the character of the apostle Paul, as his whole history shows. While his deep humility led him to regard himself as "less than the least of all saints;" yet that humility was combined with a high sense of the dignity of his office and work, as an ambassador of heaven who was appointed to "preach among the Gentiles the unsearchable riches of Christ." But though he regarded himself as a humble "servant of Christ," and "the servant of his people for Jesus' sake," yet he would never stoop to be "the servant of men," by humouring their prejudices, or flattering their passions, or employing unworthy means to gain their favour or applause. When assailed by his enemies, he displayed a dignity of bearing, a calmness of spirit, and a resolute assertion of his rights, which showed that he did not fear the face of man, and that he would not submit to be trampled upon, or treated with injustice. Thus, for instance, at Philippi, after he had been cruelly beaten and thrust into the prison, and when the magistrates found out next morning that they had committed a great wrong, and sent to tell him that he might depart, Paul stood firmly upon his rights as a Roman citizen, and said, "They have beaten us openly uncondemned, being Romans; and now do they thrust us out privily? nay verily; but let them come themselves and fetch us out." Again, when he was put upon his trial before Festus at Cæsarea, and when the governor, instead of declaring him innocent of the charge, as he believed him to be, urged him to undergo a new trial before his enemies at Jerusalem, the apostle replied, with calm dignity, "I stand at

Cæsar's judgment-seat, where I ought to be judged: to the Jews have I done no wrong, as thou very well knowest. For if I be an offender, or have committed anything worthy of death, I refuse not to die: but if there be none of these things whereof these accuse me, no man may deliver me unto them. *I appeal unto Cæsar.*" Nor can we forget his dignified bearing in the presence of Felix, when the apostle "reasoned of righteousness, temperance, and judgment to come," with such thrilling eloquence and power, that the judge "trembled" before his prisoner. Such calm self-possession and bold independence indicated not only conscious innocence, but also the highest moral dignity.

Then, also, this high elevation of character appears in his utter indifference to human applause. Though he sought to commend himself, or rather his message, to every man's conscience in the sight of God, and to please every man for his good to edification—and though he was not insensible to the favourable opinion of the wise and good—yet he was entirely free from that thirst for notoriety and that love of applause, which are characteristic of small and vulgar minds. He never shunned to declare the whole counsel of God, from the fear of giving offence to gainsayers. Nor did he spare even his best friends, when their conduct was worthy of blame, but he rebuked them sharply. A remarkable instance of this occurred at

Antioch, where he withstood even the apostle Peter to the face, because he had "not walked uprightly, according to the truth of the Gospel," by giving countenance to those who attached undue importance to ceremonial observances. And when the Galatians took offence, because he had reproved them for their ritualism, he refused to made any concession or apology; and he repeated his rebuke in the strongest terms, saying, "Am I, therefore, become your enemy, because I tell you the truth?" Similar to this was that noble and touching appeal which he made to the Thessalonians, and which reveals so clearly the high motives which uniformly influenced his whole conduct: "As we were allowed to be put in trust with the Gospel, so we speak; not as pleasing men, but God, who trieth our hearts. For neither at any time used we flattering words, as ye know, nor a cloak of covetousness; God is witness! nor of men sought we glory, neither of you, nor yet of others." As an eloquent writer has said, "He must be fond of applause indeed, who sighs for that which has been lavishly sprinkled on the most worthless, who is willing to be made a king to-day at the expense of being stoned to-morrow, who glories in being now saluted as a god, at the risk of being anon devoured by the worms that worship him." From such weakness and meanness Paul's noble and independent spirit was entirely free. He would not stoop to curry favour with any; and he regarded with utter indifference the empty applause of the fickle multitude, as well as their groundless censure.

As another illustration of the moral dignity of his character, we may notice his entire freedom from selfish and sordid motives. He could truly say to all the churches he had planted, "I seek not yours, but you:" "I have coveted no man's silver, or gold, or apparel." He insisted indeed upon his right to temporal support from those to whom he had imparted spiritual things; but when he learned that some in the Corinthian church, were so mean spirited as to grudge their "carnal things," he scorned to receive their gifts, and chose rather to work with his own hands for his subsistence, and to accept that aid from the Macedonian churches which ought to have been given by those to whom he was ministering at the time. To show them how groundless their suspicions were, he said, "I robbed other churches, taking wages of them, to do you service." There was no robbery in the case, for these other churches, especially that of Philippi, sent their gifts to him spontaneously and cheerfully, otherwise he would not have received them at all. His meaning evidently was, that he accepted from these other churches the contributions which ought, in right and justice, to have been given by the Corinthians, as a small token of their gratitude for the spiritual blessings which he had been the means of imparting to them, as their spiritual father. But he scorned to take a farthing from them, because they basely suspected his motives; and because he wished still "*to do them service*," as a preacher of the Gospel, by disarming them of their groundless prejudices against him and his teaching.

Such, then, was the apostle Paul; and in this combination of deep humility with high moral dignity, we have an instance of the power of living Christianity which has never been surpassed, and rarely if ever equalled, by any mere man. May such instances be multiplied in the Church of these latter days, and especially among our young men. What an increase of moral power and beneficial influence would thus be secured in the Church! and what blessed results might be expected to flow from her efforts to subdue the world to Christ! and how truly might the words of the venerable apostle John be applied to those who are soon to supply the vacant places of the fathers of the Church, "I have written unto you, young men, because ye are strong, and the Word of God abideth in you, and ye have overcome the Wicked One."

CHAPTER III.

LARGE-HEARTEDNESS AND TENDER-HEARTEDNESS.

"O ye Corinthians, . . . our heart is enlarged."
—2 COR. vi. 11.

THESE words of the apostle suggest two additional and prominent features of his character, to the illustration of which we propose to devote this chapter, viz., *his large-heartedness, combined with warm or tender heartedness.*

At the time when he wrote these words, there was considerable coldness, and even alienation of affection from him, on the part of many in the Corinthian church; caused, however, not by any evil he had done to them, but by his ministerial faithfulness in reproving their errors and sins. They took offence at his plainness of speech, and his just severity of rebuke; and they counted him their enemy, because he had told them the truth, from a sincere desire to benefit their souls. This led him to fear lest, after all the labour he had bestowed upon them, and all the instructions he had given them, they should "receive the grace of God in vain." Accordingly, after recounting some of the trials which he had endured for their sakes, and the spiritual blessings which he had been instrumental in imparting to them, "making many rich," he proceeded to assure them, that however cold their affection to him might be, yet his affection to them was not in the least diminished; and that all the "straitening" in their mutual intercourse existed, not in him, but in themselves. With a heart full of unabated love, and unquenchable zeal for their highest interests, he said, "O ye Corinthians, our mouth is open unto you," to tell you your faults, and turn you from sin, and restore you to the paths of righteousness; but it is more in sorrow than in anger that we thus speak. Ye are my spiritual children, and though, as a father, I have been compelled to correct and chasten you, yet it is the very depth and warmth of my affection for you that have led me to use the rod; for *"our heart is enlarged"* with an intense desire for your spiritual good.

Let us then contemplate the character of Paul in the two aspects we have indicated.

I. LARGE-HEARTEDNESS.

There are many good and kind-hearted men who cannot be considered as great or large hearted; but Paul was distinguished by both of these qualities; and he exhibited especially a *moral* greatness and

Large-Heartedness. 35

elevation of soul, which raised him far above everything that was mean, or envious, or narrow-minded. Not that he was puffed up with pride or self-conceit; for these are the vices of men who have small minds and slender attainments. Great though he was, he bore himself like one who was quite unconscious of his greatness, and who did not care what the world thought of him. With his unaffected humility and unobtrusive modesty, there was combined a nobility of soul, a lofty magnanimity, which rendered him incapable of an unworthy action, and inspired him with the most generous emotions, and urged him to great and heroic deeds. It has been truly said, that when the anointing oil was poured on the head of the first king of Israel, a remarkable change was wrought upon his character. Samuel said to him, "The Spirit of the Lord will come upon thee, and thou shalt prophesy with them, and shalt be turned into another man," and then, it is added, "it was so, when he had turned his back to go from Samuel, God *gave him another heart*," that is a large, generous, heroic spirit, to qualify him for his kingly office. Thus, when God calls any one to do a great work, He endows His chosen servant with the needed qualifications; and this was still more emphatically true of Saul of Tarsus. When the Spirit of the Lord came upon him, in the plenitude not only of miraculous gifts, but of saving grace, God gave him also *another heart;* and endowed him with high capacities, inspired him with noble aims, and fired him with a generous ambition to devote his energies, not only to the salvation of his own countrymen, but to the evangelisation of the world. "I am a debtor," he said, "both to the Greeks and to the Barbarians, both to the wise and the unwise." Truly, his "heart was enlarged."

But to come more to particulars, his large-heartedness appears :

1. *In forming the noblest aims and purposes.*—His enlarged heart panted for the salvation of every human being, and embraced all the world in the wide circle of its generous sympathy. No distinction of sect or party, of class or colour, checked the outflow of his gushing benevolence, or chilled the fervour of his glowing zeal. He rose superior to the narrow prejudices of the Jew, and to the intense bigotry of the Pharisee. His fellow-countrymen, with scarcely an exception, vainly imagined that they were the exclusive favourites of Heaven; and they could not endure that their peculiar privileges, as the chosen people, should be shared or enjoyed by the other nations of the world. Misunderstanding the numerous predictions of their own prophets, in which the conversion of the Gentile nations is so clearly foretold, they accounted the Gentiles as hopeless outcasts from the favour of God, and considered them to be as unworthy of the children's bread as the dogs under the

A noble Aim.

master's table. Now, in these narrow and deep-rooted prejudices, Paul himself had been educated at the feet of Gamaliel, as well as under the roof of his parents; and of this, if he could ever forget it, he could not fail to be forcibly reminded on one special and trying occasion, in Jerusalem itself. When he stood on the stairs of the fortress of Antonia, and made his defence before the Jewish people, who had driven him out of the temple, and would have put him to death, unless the Roman officer had rescued him, they listened patiently to his touching appeal, until he spoke of his mission to the Gentiles. Then, however, their pent-up wrath burst forth in a torrent of violence and abuse; and "they cried out, and cast off their clothes, and threw dust into the air," shouting, "Away with such a fellow from the earth; for it is not fit that he should live." Such, in the days of his own ignorance and unbelief, had been his own feeling, when he reckoned the admission of an uncircumcised Gentile as a foul profanation of the Church of God.

How great then in this respect was the change which had been wrought upon him by Divine grace. Now he gloried in being the "Apostle of the Gentiles;" and his whole soul was devoted to their salvation. "Unto me," he said, "who am less than the least of all saints, is this grace given, that I should preach among the Gentiles the unsearchable riches of Christ."

Never did the love of fame impel the statesman more powerfully to self-sacrificing toil, nor the love of country impel the patriot to deeds of heroism, nor the love of glory impel the soldier to fight on the battle-field, nor the love of science impel the student to spend laborious days and sleepless nights in quest of some new discovery, than the *love of souls* impelled the apostle to turn them from darkness to light, and to win them to Christ. We justly admire the old patriots and heroes of Greece and Rome, although with their love of country there was mingled, in no small degree, the love of distinction and the thirst for earthly glory and human applause. But the "Apostle of the Gentiles" was fired with a far nobler and purer ambition—the ambition of turning many to righteousness, and making them jewels in the Redeemer's crown; and of him it might truly be said, that he was "above ambition great." His greatness consisted, not in desiring to be thought great, but in his intense love of that which is truly great and essentially noble and excellent. He was free from all selfish aims; and what he chiefly sought was, not his own things, but the things of others, and especially "the things which are Jesus Christ's," and the advancement of His glory in the salvation of men. Truly his "heart was enlarged" to all the world: and rapid as his movements were from place to place, yet they were far "outrun by the celerity of his desires." The key to this part of his character is thus furnished by himself: "Though I be free from all men, yet have I made myself servant unto all, that I might gain the more. And unto the Jews I became as a Jew, that I might gain the Jews. To them that are without law, as without law, that I might gain them that are without law. To the weak became I as weak, that I might gain the weak: I am made all things to all men, that I might by all means save some. And this I do for the Gospel's sake." Here then is a model for young men, which they would do well to copy closely, by cherishing lofty aims and purposes, by honouring all men, and doing good to all as they have opportunity. In thus feeling and acting, in rising above self and sense and time, and in devoting their energies to the welfare of souls, they will know by experience the truth of those words of the Lord Jesus —"It is more blessed to give than to receive."

2. *In prosecuting his labours for more than thirty years amid formidable difficulties and dangers.*—Many begin to run well who never reach the mark or win the prize; or to use a homely expression, "Many put on their spurs who never ride." Many have commenced a good work or a noble enterprise with sanguine hope, and even with high enthusiasm; but when difficulties met them in the way, when strenuous opposition was to be encountered, and painful sacrifices were to be endured, they soon lost heart, and fled from the post of duty in despair. How often, alas!

have the promising blossoms of early piety been withered into dust, by worldly companionship, and the bitter blasts of temptation. How often have promising young men been tossed about by every wind of doctrine, and every wave of passion, instead of standing "faithful among the faithless," like a rock that resists the fury of the storm. Many have begun to build, but not counting the cost, were not able to finish. Many have put on, or seemed to put on, the Christian armour, who have suffered an inglorious defeat in the battle with sin. And to such the caution of the King of Israel is most appropriate, "Let not him that girdeth on his harness boast himself, as he that putteth it off." To persevere in the path of duty, and in the walk of Christian benevolence amid opposition and obloquy, amid hardship and sacrifice, amid danger and death—this requires no ordinary strength of principle, and no small measure of *enlargement* and devotion of soul.

A very striking parallel has been drawn, by one of our greatest preachers, between the position of a modern missionary, and the position of the apostle Paul, in going forth to convert the nations. We cannot but admire the large-heartedness of those, in modern times, who leave their home and their friends to dwell among savages, and who take, as it were, their lives in their hand to extend the peaceful triumphs of the Cross, in the dark places of the earth. And yet, painful as are the sacrifices which they are required to make, and formidable as are the difficulties which they must encounter, they can scarcely be compared, except in a few rare instances, with those of the great apostle. One of the most striking of these exceptions is, perhaps, the illustrious Livingstone, who in his large-heartedness, seems to approach nearest to the high standard of Paul. Among his last words, as recorded in his journal, is this memorable utterance: "The spirit of missions is the spirit of our Master—the very genius of His religion. A diffusive philanthropy is Christianity itself. It requires perpetual propagation to attest its genuineness." And how impressive and touching are the words, which he wrote, in reference to slavery, a year before his death, and which are now inscribed on the tablet erected to his memory beside his grave: "All I can add in my loneliness is, may Heaven's rich blessing come down on every one, American, English, or Turk, who will help to heal the open sore of the world." This was genuine largeness of heart, and it well deserves our highest admiration. But, excepting cases like these, the average missionary in modern times, when he goes forth among the heathen, leaves behind him many Christian friends who are deeply interested in his progress and success, who sustain him with their counsel and prayers, and who will gladly welcome him on his return. Such encouragements, however, were in a great measure denied to Paul; and he was often left alone in his arduous struggles. When a prisoner at Rome, "Demas," he said, "hath forsaken me, having loved this present world." And when he was brought before the emperor, to be tried for his life, he had reason to say, "At my first answer, no man stood with me; but all men forsook me." Even his own countrymen were his greatest enemies; and he found them, in every city he visited, to be the ringleaders in almost every persecution which he endured. There was no earthly protector to whom he could look, and the Saviour, whom he preached, was "a stumbling-block to the Jews," and "foolishness to the Greeks." The obstacles which he had to contend with, in the jealousy of despotic rulers, in the pride of self-sufficient philosophers, in the bigotry of interested priests, and in the ignorance and superstition of a licentious and bloodthirsty populace, were such as would have made an ordinary man's courage quail, and caused the most hopeful to renounce his calling in despair. What elevation of soul, then, must he have possessed, to enable him to bear up, and persevere, amid such overwhelming difficulties. As has been truly said by the preacher just referred to, "it required a soul raised to a high pitch, not by sudden impressions and the force of a heated imagination, but by enlightened and steady principles; a soul wound up in all its faculties, intellectual and moral; regulated, balanced,

An ardent pursuit of it. 43

sustained, and furnished with a spring which could bear the severest pressure, which would not wear itself away by its own motion, nor suffer derangement from the changes of external circumstances; a soul exalted above the world, and all those worldly motives by which men are ordinarily actuated, attracted, or impelled; and disengaged from all selfishness, effeminacy, envy, illiberality, and those narrow prejudices which are founded on the distinction of nations, classes, and conditions in life; a soul filled with supreme love to God, and ardent love to man, fired with heavenly ambition to advance the Divine glory in the highest, and promote the eternal welfare of mankind; and which, in pursuing this noble object, was prepared to make all sacrifices, sustain all fatigues, run all hazards, endure all sufferings. And such was the soul of Paul. At the call of God, he went forth into the world, bearing (it was all his armour) the name of the Lord Jesus,— not knowing whither he went, but prepared to go wherever Providence pointed the way, to the north, the south, the east, or the west; and not knowing what would befall him, nor moved by the warnings which he received, in every city, that bonds and imprisonments awaited him. His *heart was enlarged* to all the world, and he trusted to his Master to open before him the door of faith, and to preserve him as long as He had services for him to perform." What a noble model is this for our young men! teaching them not only to begin great and good works, but to go through with them, and to do them with all their might. Instead of growing weary in well-doing, let them be steadfast, unmovable, always abounding in the work of the Lord. For "no man having put his hand to the plough, and looking back, is fit for the kingdom of God;" but "the righteous shall hold on his way, and he that hath clean hands shall be stronger and stronger."

3. *In his generous treatment of offenders.*—Of this we have one remarkable proof, in that fervent unquenchable love, which he bore towards his own unbelieving countrymen, notwithstanding their persistent enmity to him, and their repeated attempts upon his life. It is hard to love our bitterest enemies, and harder still to return good for evil; and nothing but grace, in a large measure, can enable any man to do it. But Paul did it, even to the last, heaping coals of fire upon their heads, and repaying their curses with blessings, and their persecutions with prayers. He had "great heaviness and continual sorrow in his heart," on account of the sad spiritual condition of Israel; and he could even have wished himself to be "separated from Christ," if that would have saved his brethren; so that he could say, as in the sight of the great Searcher of hearts, "My heart's desire and prayer to God for Israel is, that they might be saved."

But not to dwell upon this obvious proof of his

large-heartedness, look at his generous treatment of offenders in the Christian Church. His large heart could take in the concerns of "all the churches which he had planted." "Who is weak," he said, "and I am not weak? who is offended, and I burn not?" Read his two epistles to the Corinthian church, which owed its existence, under God, to his ministry, and which was indebted to him for all its Christian privileges and hopes; but which, yielding to the influence of false teachers, was soon estranged from its benefactor, and embracing fatal errors and falling into gross sins, required the rod of painful discipline, and sharp rebuke, to heal their backslidings. But in all his rebukes of their sins, how tender and intense was his love to their souls. And when his rebukes had produced the designed effect of leading them to repentance, how readily and frankly did he forgive them for all their unkind thoughts, and ungenerous suspicions of himself; and how completely and joyfully did he take them back into his friendship and confidence. During the interval between his first and second epistles, he purposely remained for a time at Ephesus, on the opposite shore of the Egean Sea, lest his personal presence at that time should add fuel to the flame of contention at Corinth. At length, in his perplexity and anxiety, he moved northward to Troas, hoping to meet Titus there, and to hear tidings of the Corinthian church. But though "a door was opened to him of the Lord" at Troas, he had no heart to preach, and he says, "I had no rest in my spirit, because I found not Titus my brother; but taking my leave of them, I went from thence into Macedonia." There, at last, the wished-for tidings reached him that the Corinthians had repented of their sin, and returned to their first love; and he gave utterance to his exuberant joy, in these words of generous affection and all-embracing charity, "O ye Corinthians, our mouth is open unto you, our heart is enlarged." No cold constraint, no distance, nor reserve, nor alienation now. The ice has melted under the genial heat, and there are now gushing streams of affection, and welling fountains of gladness. "Great," he said, "is my boldness of speech towards you, great is my glorying of you: I am filled with comfort, I am exceeding joyful in all our tribulation." Yes, it is the glory of a Christian to pass over an offence, and frankly to forgive injuries and insults. It is the glory of a man of the world to resent injuries, and return evil for evil, to harbour secret grudges, and never to forget an insult. But, if our hearts are "enlarged" with a sense of God's forgiving love, we shall be constrained to treat even our enemies, as God has treated us. Let all, and especially young men, imitate Paul in his *large-heartedness*, by laying aside all narrow prejudices, all ungenerous suspicions and uncharitable judgments, and by manifesting in their whole conduct the elevating and expansive power of a living Christianity.

II. WARM OR TENDER HEARTEDNESS.

The combination, in a high degree, of the two qualities of the great and the gentle, of the lofty and the tender, constitutes the highest moral excellence. But the combination of both in the same person, in equal strength, is comparatively rare. On the one hand, *large-heartedness* or elevation of soul, if possessed alone, has a tendency to isolate a man from his fellows, and to alienate their sympathies, even while kindling their admiration; as we admire at a distance a magnificent mountain, whose summit is covered with perpetual snow. And on the other hand, *tender-heartedness*, if possessed alone, has a tendency to degenerate into moral weakness and lachrymose sentimentalism. But when the two qualities are combined in a high degree of strength, their possessor, though towering like a mountain above the clouds, sends down, even from the diadem of snow, gushing streams of melting sympathy and love, to refresh the thirsty valleys, and clothe them with verdure and gladness.

In the apostle Paul, the two qualities were admirably combined. He had not only a large but a loving heart. While it was large enough to embrace the world, it was sympathetic enough to feel for every woe, and to identify itself with every child of sorrow. He could truly say to his converts, "We were gentle among you, even as a nurse cherisheth her children; so, being affectionately desirous of you, we were willing to have imparted unto you, not the Gospel of God only, but also our own souls, because ye were dear unto us."

There is a sermon by one of the greatest of modern preachers upon "the tears of St Paul;" and he notices the fact that, in his farewell address at Miletus to the elders of the Ephesian church, the apostle refers to his tears no less than three times. First, he had shed *tears of suffering;* as when he says that, while he was with them, he had "served the Lord with all humility of mind, and *with many tears* and temptations." Then he had shed *tears of sympathy;* as when it is said that, at the final parting on the seashore, after he had prayed, "they *all wept sore.*" And further, he *shed tears of pastoral solicitude;* as when he says that, "by the space of three years I ceased not to warn every one, day and night, *with tears.*" This tender-heartedness showed how closely Paul was conformed to his Divine Master; for He too shed tears of suffering in Gethsemane, when He "offered up prayers and supplications with strong crying and *tears;*" and He shed tears of sympathy with the sorrowing sisters of Bethany at their brother's grave; and He also shed tears of pastoral solicitude, when He *wept* over Jerusalem's guilt, and impenitence, and impending ruin. Let us then turn our thoughts for a little to these evidences of Paul's warm or tender heartedness.

1. *There were tears of suffering.*—He was not like the proud Stoic, who thought it a meritorious thing to suppress natural feeling or painful emotion; and he did not affect to be cold and impassive under his manifold afflictions, nor attempt to "stifle the expressions of a grief which he could not help feeling, and which he could not conceal without dissimulation." Nor was he a man of robust frame or of iron mould; but he had a sickly body and a sensitive spirit; and he had "a thorn in the flesh," which caused him great suffering, and for the removal of which he besought the Lord thrice. And though he had high moral courage, yet he was not remarkable for mere physical courage. Like his Master, he naturally and instinctively shrank from pain, and was often cast down by fear, greatly depressed in spirit, and much grieved by the ingratitude and desertion of his friends. "I was with you," he says, "in weakness, and in fear, and in much trembling;" and again, "without were fightings, within were fears." Yes, it cost Paul much to be a Christian; and he had to bear a heavy cross of suffering; and many were the tears he shed—not tears of impatience or fretfulness, but tears of anguish and sore affliction.

2. *There were tears of sympathy.*—In almost every page of his epistles, he expresses his strong affection for his friends and fellow-labourers, and the great enjoyment which he experienced in their society, and the sorrow which he felt in their absence; and especially when any of them, like Demas, turned their backs upon him. For the comfort, and even for the prejudices of his converts, he showed the tenderest consideration; and treated them with a uniform courtesy and kindliness, which betokened a peculiarly warm and loving heart. His tender attachment to "Luke, the beloved physician," to Timothy, his "own son in the faith," and to Titus his other son; and his mention by name of so many of those who had ministered to his wants, and helped him in his labours; and his cordial greetings of them at the close of his epistles—all this indicates the warmth of his friendship, and the tenderness and depth of his sympathetic love to his brethren and sisters in the Lord.

3. *There were also tears of pastoral solicitude.*—Day and night he had warned the Ephesian church "with tears" against prevailing errors and sins. And in reminding the Philippians of those "enemies of the Cross of Christ," "whose god was their belly, and whose glory was in their shame," he says, "I now tell you, *even weeping*." Then to the Thessalonians he says, "As ye know how we exhorted and comforted,

and charged every one of you (as a father doth his children), that ye would walk worthy of God, who hath called you unto His kingdom and glory." And then when he received "good tidings of their faith and charity," and of their earnest "desire to see him, as we also to see you," he was filled with comfort and joy; "for now," says he, "we live if ye stand fast in the Lord," as if his very existence depended upon their steadfastness in the faith and holiness of the Gospel. Such also, as we have seen, was his warm affection for the Corinthian church, and his earnest pastoral solicitude for their spiritual welfare. And does not this show, that while his "heart was enlarged" to all the world, yet it was also a most tender, kind, and loving heart?

In all this, then, what a bright pattern is exhibited for the imitation of young men! Their future comfort and welfare depend much upon their setting before them a lofty aim or ideal, and then resolutely following it out, and striving to realise it, in their personal character and conduct. In the admirable address of the Moderator,* at the close of the Free Church Assembly, it was truly said, "Every man becomes like the object of his strongest love and highest admiration, and if a man admires, and trusts, and loves his own vile self, he becomes in every way vile. The one absolutely beautiful object ever

* Dr Moody Stuart in 1875.

disclosed on this earth of ours, is Jesus Christ, wholly admirable from His cradle to His cross, and even those who are not His friends admire His peerless beauty." We must, however, not only admire, but imitate Him; and though we cannot hope in this life to reach His high standard of moral perfection, yet in looking to those, such as Paul, who were made like Him, we are encouraged to hope that what grace did for them, it can do for us. Let us never forget that the Gospel is designed, not only to give peace and comfort to the troubled conscience, and rest to the weary soul, but also to elevate and ennoble our whole character, and so to "enlarge our hearts," as that we shall "run in the way of God's commandments," even amid trials and temptations, and in danger and death. And let us not forget that true happiness consists, not only in having real fellowship with God, but also in the exercise of holy love, in the interchange of pure affection, and in the doing of generous deeds. It consists, to no small extent, in large-heartedness and kind-heartedness toward all men. When we are invited, as sinners, to come to Christ, it is not only for the purpose of being saved ourselves, but also for the purpose of becoming blessings to others, and seeking their salvation. Who ever heard of a deist or infidel weeping because his doctrine was rejected? But Paul wept when his doctrine was rejected by some and perverted by others. It grieved him to the heart, and his grief found vent in bitter tears of sorrow. Such is living Christianity, for it leads us to look not merely on our own things, but also on the things of others.

> "Wherever in the world I am,
>   In whatsoe'er estate,
> I have a fellowship with hearts
>   To keep and cultivate;
> And a work of lowly love to do
>   For the Lord on whom I wait."

CHAPTER IV.

UNSELFISHNESS AND CONSCIENTIOUSNESS.

"I seek not yours, but you."—2 COR. xii. 14.

THESE words of the apostle suggest two additional features in his character, which we propose to consider in combination, according to the plan already indicated, viz., his *transparent unselfishness* united with *unswerving conscientiousness*. He was entirely free from selfish and sordid motives; and no one could ever say or imagine that he sought to make a gain of godliness. If any one, and especially if a minister, were to seek merely his own profit and pleasure, he would soon lose all his moral weight, and destroy his ministerial influence. No doubt he is entitled to his temporal support from those to whom he ministers; and this, not as a matter of charity, but as a matter of right, for "the labourer is worthy of his hire;" and it is for their own interest to make such arrangements, as will relieve him from the burden of worldly cares and anxieties, and enable him, as far as they can, to devote himself wholly to his proper work. But still

Unselfishness.

his main object must be the spiritual good of those committed to his charge, their personal union to Christ, and their progressive advancement in all Christian excellence; so that he may be enabled truly to say to them, without the fear of contradiction, "*I seek not yours, but you.*"

I. UNSELFISHNESS.

The spirit of selfishness is deeply imbedded in our fallen nature; it forms the very essence of our moral depravity, and is the prolific source of almost every sin. When the love of God, that cardinal and controlling principle, was expelled from the human heart, the love of self rushed in to occupy the void; and hence it is, that self-conceit, self-righteousness, self-reliance, and self-indulgence, have become the prominent characteristics of fallen humanity. Instead of giving glory to God, man naturally strives to be a god to himself, and to make his own interests, and designs, and wishes, his chief good and the great end of his existence. The main questions, which occupy his mind, and call forth his energies, are not, How shall I honour Christ? or glorify God? or benefit my fellow-men?—but rather, What shall I eat? what shall I drink? wherewithal shall I be clothed? how shall I gain wealth, or secure the greatest amount of pleasure, or make to myself a name in the world?

Now, wherever this selfishness predominates in the

soul, it causes unspeakable misery to its victim, and great injury to society. It makes a man restless, dissatisfied, and unhappy; and it sets him against his brother, and produces a callous indifference to his rights and interests. It is the spirit of him who said, "Am I my brother's keeper?" and if this spirit were indulged universally and without restraint, it would change the world into a pandemonium of lawless lust and ruthless violence. Even in good men, the manifestations of this spirit are not always nor entirely suppressed; and how many humbling discoveries of it have been seen in their actions. When they do a right thing, how often is it done to be seen of men, to magnify self, and to gain the world's favour or flattery? Many have done generous deeds, and conferred signal benefits on their fellow-creatures, especially in our own day; and we ought to be thankful for this, and give them full credit for the best of motives. But in so far as they have been enabled to "do good by stealth, and blush to find it fame," they themselves would be the first to acknowledge that it was not nature, but grace, that had brought them up to this high standard. Paul himself had frequent and sad experience of selfishness, in the conduct even of his own friends; for when requesting his beloved Timothy to be sent to him, he said, "I have no man like-minded; for *all seek their own*, not the things which are Jesus Christ's." And even yet, the same spirit prevails in the Church to a melancholy extent; for doth not the Spirit say expressly, that "*in the last days* perilous times shall come; for men shall *be lovers of their own selves?*"

We may be sure, therefore, that if Paul himself manifested a spirit of unselfishness, this was not natural to him, but was acquired by grace, and was the fruit of the operation of the Holy Spirit in his heart. Having received the Spirit of Christ, he had also, in no ordinary degree, the mind of Christ. In respect of disinterestedness, the Master, of course, stands pre-eminent and alone; and none could ever say, with the same degree of truth, "I seek not mine own glory," and "I seek not mine own will, but the will of Him who hath sent me." Let us see then how far the servant resembled his Master, in his freedom from selfishness, and from all worldly designs and interests.

1. Paul's unselfishness appears in renouncing all his worldly advantages and prospects for Christ. In embracing a religion which was everywhere spoken against, he had nothing of a worldly kind to gain, but he had everything to lose. He had to give up all his early friendships, and all the respect and reputation which he had won by his superior gifts and attainments, and all the alluring prospects of worldly advancement and honour, which were held out to him, as a disciple in the school of Gamaliel, as an adherent of those in power, and as one who had "profited in the Jews' religion above many his equals." And not only so,

but as we have already seen, he had to enter upon a life of intense suffering, of incessant self-denial, of imminent peril, and appalling persecution. All this he knew full well, for he had been forewarned of it; but he did not for an instant shrink from the sacrifice. Having counted the cost, he was willing to pay it, and he did pay it to the full, as long as he lived. Like the other apostles, he "forsook all, and followed Christ," during his whole lifetime; in the storm, as well as in the calm; in gloom, as well as in sunshine; through bad report, as well as through good report. "None of these things," he said, "move me, neither count I my life dear unto myself, so that I might finish my course with joy, and the ministry, which I have received of the Lord Jesus, to testify the gospel of the grace of God." "What things were gain to me, those I counted loss for Christ. Yea doubtless, and I count all things but loss for the excellency of the knowledge of Christ Jesus my Lord; for whom I have suffered the loss of all things." These are noble utterances, breathing a spirit of the highest disinterestedness; and they are made not boastfully, but most humbly and truthfully. Such is the spirit of living Christianity; and wherever it is felt in its power, it cannot but expel the spirit of selfishness, and constrain us to look not merely on our own things, but also upon the things of others, and to sacrifice our time, and ease, and comfort, for their spiritual benefit.

2. Paul's unselfishness appears in refusing his temporal support from niggardly churches. One of these was the church of Corinth, which had been planted by himself. In his second epistle, he tells them, that during his former visit, he had not been "burdensome to them;" and he tells them, further, that though he was about to visit them again, yet he was determined to act on the same principle. "I will not," he says, "be burdensome to you; for I seek not yours, but you." The reason why he acted thus was, because certain false teachers had persuaded many of his converts that he was influenced by mercenary motives, and that he wished to make money by preaching the Gospel. At that time there was a number of itinerant teachers, who went about the cities of Greece to lecture "for filthy lucre's sake;" teaching erroneous doctrines, poisoning the minds of the converts, causing divisions in the Church, and striving to undermine the apostle's influence over his spiritual children. These false teachers, whose only object was to enrich themselves, by flattering the prejudices and pandering to the low tastes and passions of their hearers, sought to impute the same base design to the apostle; and strange to say, they often succeeded in gaining for a time a greater ascendency over the minds of some, than Paul himself obtained. Accordingly, in a strain of severe but friendly irony, he reproved the Corinthians for allowing themselves to become the silly dupes of

these selfish and designing men, "who made a gain of godliness." "For," he says, "ye suffer fools gladly, seeing ye yourselves are wise. For ye suffer, if a man bring you into bondage, if a man devour you, if a man take of you, if a man exalt himself, if a man smite you on the face" (2 Cor. xi. 19, 20). Thus these false teachers were far more popular at Corinth than Paul himself was. He was too strict and uncompromising, in his principles and conduct, to suit the taste or gain the applause of weakly and *low-set* believers. He would not stoop to their low level, or minister to their carnal pride and self-conceit; but as the false teachers willingly did so, they gained great influence over vulgar minds, and got large sums of money.

Now, it was in these circumstances that Paul refused to take anything from the Corinthians for his temporal support; because he knew that if he did, his motives would be misunderstood and misrepresented. Therefore he wrought with his own hands at the trade of tent-making, in order that he might preserve his independence and authority as a servant of Christ, and let all men see that he was not influenced by selfish or sordid motives, in preaching the Gospel to them, and that he sought not *theirs* but *them;* not their money, but their souls; their salvation from sin, and their highest spiritual advantage. Hence that noble appeal: "Have I committed an offence in abasing myself, that ye might be exalted, because I have preached to you the Gospel of God *freely?* I robbed other churches, taking wages of them, to do you service. And when I was present with you, and wanted, I was chargeable to no man: for that which was lacking to me the brethren who came from Macedonia supplied; and in all things I have kept myself from being burdensome unto you, and *so will I keep myself.* As the truth of Christ is in me, no man shall stop me of this boasting in the regions of Achaia. Wherefore? because I love you not? God knoweth. But what I do, that I will do, that I may cut off occasion from them which desire occasion; that wherein they glory, they may be found even as we. For such are false apostles, deceitful workers, transforming themselves into the apostles of Christ" (2 Cor. xi. 7-13).

Such then was the unselfishness of the great apostle in the matter of money; and he could confidently appeal to all the churches, as he did to the elders of the Ephesian church, in these memorable words: "I have coveted no man's silver, or gold, or apparel. Yea, ye yourselves know that these hands have ministered unto my necessities, and to them that were with me." Rather than allow his usefulness to be marred, and the progress of the Gospel to be hindered, he positively refused to take one farthing for his temporal support from niggardly churches, although it was their duty to give it, and his right to receive it. But surely it said little for *them*, that they should have been so suspicious of his motives, as to compel him to have recourse to exhausting manual labour, and to work as a common tradesman for his daily bread. Had these churches been more generous in contributing to his support, they might have had more of his time devoted to their instruction than it was possible for him to give; and they would have spared his loving heart many a bitter pang on account of their churlishness, and would have encouraged and cheered him in his arduous and manifold labours for their spiritual and eternal welfare. Niggardliness in supporting and spreading the Gospel is both a selfish and a short-sighted policy. It brings a blight upon the soul, and a curse upon our worldly possessions. It secularises and degrades a man, and prevents him from receiving much benefit from the means of grace. It sears the conscience, and hardens the heart, like the simoom of the desert, where little rain ever falls, and where, when it does fall, it is at once absorbed in the sand, and never sends forth even a tiny rill to water and refresh the thirsty ground. "There is that scattereth, and yet increaseth; and there is that withholdeth more than is meet, but it tendeth to poverty. The liberal soul shall be made fat; and he that watereth shall be watered also himself." Let young men especially cultivate and practically manifest a liberal and generous spirit; and in doing so they will open up sources of enduring happiness to themselves, and be the instruments of extensive blessing to others. God is always giving, and never needs anything from us. He opens His liberal hand, and satisfies the desire of every living thing. It is God-like to give; and let us "be followers of God, as dear children;" "remembering the words of the Lord Jesus, how He said, It is more blessed to give than to receive."

It should here be noticed, however, that while Paul refused, in certain cases, to receive his temporal support from those to whom he ministered, yet he asserted very strongly his right to that support. He did not hold up his example, in this respect, as one that all other ministers must imitate; and neither did he think that it is any degradation to them to receive temporal things, in return for spiritual things. On the contrary, he plainly declared, "So hath the Lord ordained, that they who preach the Gospel should live of the Gospel." And still more expressly he said, "Let him that is taught in the Word communicate to him that teacheth, in all good things." The teacher may waive his right to this, on grounds of Christian expediency; but the right itself is sacred and unchallengeable. It would be well therefore if professing Christians would remember, what many are prone to forget, that the adequate support of a Gospel ministry is not a matter of charity or personal favour, but a matter of simple justice. It is not a boon conferred, or a deed of generosity done; but a debt paid, for service rendered and received. "If," said the apostle, "we have sown unto you spiritual things, is it a great thing if we reap your carnal things?" And those who have received the greatest spiritual benefit from the ministry of the Word, will be the last to imagine that their debt is fully discharged by their most munificent contributions.

It may be further noticed here, that while Paul refused to receive his temporal support in certain cases, yet in other cases he did accept it gladly and gratefully; especially when it was offered voluntarily, and given cheerfully, and not as the price of his independence. Though he refused the gifts of the Corinthian church, yet he willingly received them from the churches of Macedonia, and particularly from the church at Philippi, which appears to have been largely blessed with a loving heart and a liberal spirit. That church, the first fruits of his labours in Europe, was peculiarly dear to him; and the love was reciprocal, and very ardent on both sides. How touching are the words he wrote to them, in acknowledging the generous gift which they had sent to him at Rome, by a special messenger: "I rejoiced in the Lord greatly, that now at the last your care of me hath flourished again; wherein ye were also careful, but ye lacked opportunity. Not that I speak in respect of want: for I have learned, in whatsoever state I am, therewith to be content. I know both how to be abased, and I know how to abound: everywhere, and in all things, I am instructed both to be full and to be hungry, both to abound and to suffer need. I can do all things through Christ who strengtheneth me. Notwithstanding ye have well done that ye did communicate with my affliction. . . . Not because I desire a gift; but I desire fruit that may abound to your account. But I have all, and abound: I am full, having received of Epaphroditus the things which were sent from you, an odour of a sweet smell, a sacrifice acceptable, well-pleasing to God. But my God shall supply all your need according to His riches in glory by Christ Jesus" (Phil. iv. 10-19). These words of heartfelt gratitude and touching tenderness, show how cordially the apostle welcomed such love-tokens from the Philippian church. Not only were they "acceptable" to himself, but they were "well-pleasing to God;" and to Him he devoted them as "sacrifices" on His altar, or as sweet incense, the fragrance of which, as it ascended to heaven, refreshed his own spirit; while along with it, he offered up the incense of his own intercession for spiritual blessings, sufficient to "supply all their need." Would that such blessed interchanges of feeling and desire were multiplied in all the churches—pastors dealing out spiritual things faithfully to their flocks, and their flocks dealing out temporal things faithfully to them; and thus manifesting a happy co-operation, and a holy harmony, in works of faith and labours of love for the spread of the Gospel. "But this I say" (these are the apostle's words), "He who soweth sparingly shall reap also sparingly; and he who soweth bountifully shall reap also bountifully. Every man according as he purposeth in his heart, so let him give; not grudgingly, or of necessity: for God loveth a cheerful giver. And God is able to make all grace abound toward you; that ye, always having all sufficiency in all things, may abound to every good work."

3. Paul's unselfishness appears also in his deep concern for the salvation of his fellow-men. To all, he could truly say, "I seek not yours, but you." For this, he was ready to sacrifice his own ease and comfort, his health and strength, his good name, and life itself. To save souls, and promote the spiritual welfare of his converts, he counted no risk too great, and no labour too severe; and even the ingratitude and alienation of those whom he sought to bless, could not quench the ardour of his love to them, or diminish the intensity of his zeal for their good. "I will very gladly," he said, "spend and be spent for you; though the more abundantly I love you, the less I be loved."

How different is all this from the natural tendencies of man! and how nobly superior to his innate selfishness! Even sinners can love those who love them, or who shower favours upon them; but to return good for evil, and requite hatred with love, is a rare achievement. And there is a kind of religious selfishness (if we may use the expression) in which even true Christians indulge, and which prompts them to care solely for their own spiritual welfare, and to feel little concern for the salvation of others, or for the advancement of the Redeemer's kingdom. Their religion, such as it is, is confined chiefly to their own breast; and their main object, in waiting on religious ordinances, is merely to get comfort to their own minds, and not to be stimulated to zeal and active effort on behalf of others. Such is not the benevolent and expansive spirit of the Gospel. It certainly was not the spirit of the great apostle, whose love to souls constrained him to put forth all his energies for their spiritual good, and to impart to them the blessings with which he himself had been enriched and gladdened. Here, then, is a model for young men. Let them put their hands to some good work, and live and labour, not for themselves only, but for the benefit of others. Let them study to be useful in their day and generation; and seize opportunities of doing good in the sphere allotted to them, and among their friends and companions; saying, like Moses to his father-in-law, "We are journeying unto the place of which the Lord said, I will give it you: come thou with us, and we will do thee good; for the Lord hath spoken good concerning Israel." Thus it will be manifest that their souls are prospering; and they will be far happier, in giving their time, or their means, or their energies, to works of piety and charity, than the man who grasps all, and grudges every effort and sacrifice in the service of Christ. "They that be wise shall shine as the brightness of the firmament; and they that turn many to righteousness as the stars for ever and ever."

II. Unswerving Conscientiousness.

The apostle was not only generous, but he was also just. His unselfishness was tempered and regulated by a conscientious regard to principle and duty, especially in fulfilling the charge which Christ had laid upon him, so that he could say to all, "*I seek you.*" There are many men who are unselfish and generous, lavish in their expenditure, and ready even to give away what is not their own, but who are not so remarkable for strict conscientiousness. Many sad and humbling illustrations of this have been furnished in the records of mercantile affairs for many years past.

But in the apostle Paul, transparent unselfishness was combined with unswerving conscientiousness. "Herein," he said, "do I exercise myself, to have always a conscience void of offence toward God and toward men." This was the "exercise" or self-discipline which he continually practised, the moral training to which he subjected himself. Whatever his conscience condemned, he strenuously fought against, and sought grace to subdue. Even while he was unconverted, he honestly strove to obey the dictates of his conscience, though it was then unenlightened; so that he really thought he was doing God service in putting the Christians to death. Even then, his conduct was outwardly irreproachable, and entirely free from gross vices. He was not a profligate, but his conscience had power to restrain him from open sin.

But when he was converted, and when his conscience was quickened and enlightened by Divine grace and truth, he aimed at reaching, and he actually attained, a far higher standard of morality than he had ever imagined before: and there ran, through the whole texture of his subsequent life, "the one golden thread of an honest and tender conscience." In all his epistles, and especially in those to Timothy and Titus, he manifests this ruling principle of his character, and shows how highly he valued the blessing of a pure and good conscience. Thus he says, that "the end of the commandment is charity, out of a pure heart, and of a *good* conscience," that is a pacified and self-approving conscience: and solemnly he charges his beloved son to hold fast "a good conscience; which some having put away, concerning faith have made shipwreck." The importance and the blessedness of maintaining a good conscience, by doing whatever we know to be right, and by shunning whatever we know to be wrong, it is impossible to exaggerate. The neglect of known duty and the wilful indulgence of known sin produce a terribly demoralising influence upon character, by lowering the moral tone, blunting the finer sensibilities of the heart, disturbing and perverting the instincts of conscience, darkening the intellect, and confusing its perceptions of the difference between right and wrong, and leading men to call evil good, and good evil. Young men, especially, should beware of doing violence to conscience, and of acting contrary to its dictates and warnings; otherwise, they will blight even their worldly prospects, and still more, endanger or destroy their eternal interests. It has been truly said by an eminent writer, "I am convinced that open vice among us would be repressed with a firmer hand and a clearer judgment, if there were not among men of high social influence, some whose past lives have left a hollow consciousness of guilt, and therefore a secret faltering, and a weakness, which dare not rise to the Christian standard."

Paul's thorough conscientiousness appears especially in his high and quick sense of honour, with regard to money affairs. When he was the prisoner of Felix at Cæsarea, he might easily have obtained his liberty, if he could have stooped to bribe the governor with the expected gift of money. And his delicacy of conscience appears in offering to pay his friend Philemon all the loss he had sustained by the dishonesty of his runaway slave Onesimus. And still more it appears in the scrupulous exactness with which he managed all the business connected with the collecting of the contributions of the churches for the poor saints at Jerusalem. He refused to take the sole charge of the money collected, lest he should expose himself to unworthy suspicions; but he insisted that the churches themselves should choose commissioners of their own to accompany him on his errand of charity; thus acting upon his own rule, to "provide things honest, not only in the sight of the Lord, but *also in the sight of men.*"

In all this, what a noble pattern is presented to young men! How careful should they be to be strictly honest, and conscientious in all pecuniary transactions; and how earnestly should they beware of getting into debt, for it will soon get them into disgrace, and bring them to shame and ruin. Nothing tends more to degrade the character of a man, and to take off the fine edge of conscience, and to make him the helpless victim of the world's temptations, than running wilfully into debt, and failing to pay his accounts with scrupulous exactness. The sum at first may be small; but "he that is unfaithful in that which is least, will be unfaithful also in much." And not less injurious to character, and blinding to conscience, and destructive of confidence, is every kind of dishonesty and fraud in the transactions of trade. Ill-gotten gains are usually soon lost; and even when retained, they are a curse to their possessor, by debasing his character, blunting his conscience, and driving him to shifts and subterfuges which not only blight his worldly prospects, but deaden his own moral feelings, and make him an easy prey to Satan's subtle wiles. "Keep thy heart with all diligence, for out of it are the issues of life." "By what means shall a young man cleanse his way?" "By taking heed thereto, *according to Thy Word.*"

Finally, Paul's conscientiousness appears in his faithful preaching of the Gospel, and his earnest efforts to win souls to Christ. No mere man could ever more truly say, than he could, to all his hearers, "I seek not yours, but you." His great aim was to rouse them from the sleep of spiritual death, to probe their consciences to the quick, to pierce them with saving convictions of sin; and then to draw them to the Saviour of sinners, in order to be washed in His precious and peace-speaking blood, and renewed inwardly by His Holy Spirit, and so made meet for His glorious presence in heaven. In aiming at this, he did not use flattering words, but he used great "plainness of speech," and sharpness of reproof. And though many counted him their enemy "because he told them the truth," yet his conscience would not let him be silent, or allow him to keep back any part of the counsel of God, or tempt him to dilute or alter his Master's message, in order to make it more palatable to the carnal mind. And this, under the Divine blessing, was the great secret of that wonderful success which crowned his labours in the Lord's vineyard. "Necessity is laid upon me," he said; "yea, woe is unto me, if I preach not the Gospel!" "But though we, or an angel from heaven, preach any other Gospel unto you than that which we have preached unto you, let him be accursed."

Here, then, is a model for young men, which they would do well to copy, by striving to do good, and by using as their instrument and lever power that Gospel of the grace of God, which in its simplicity and purity is "the power of God unto salvation to every one that believeth." Let them therefore never be ashamed of the Gospel of Christ in these days of abounding error, and let it produce its full effect upon their own hearts and lives; so that like Paul, they may become living epistles of Christ, known and read of all men, by combining a spirit of transparent unselfishness with a spirit of unswerving conscientiousness.

In the next chapter, we shall refer to Paul's high moral courage combined with habitual prayerfulness.

CHAPTER V.

COURAGE AND PRAYERFULNESS.

"I can do all things through Christ who strengtheneth me."
—PHIL. iv. 13.

A CORRECT and complete idea of the whole is best obtained by the study of its various parts, viewed not only separately and in detail, but also in their several relations and adjustments to each other. In examining a work of art, such as a statue or a picture, we do not pronounce it to be a masterpiece of genius, however accurate it may be in its details, unless its various parts are well proportioned and harmoniously adjusted to each other, so as to produce, by their *combination*, symmetry in form and beauty in colouring. And so with human character. There may be great mental and moral excellences, but if these are combined with glaring faults or defects, we must withhold our admiration. When, however, the noblest qualities are exhibited in happy combination, and harmonious adjustment and operation, we pronounce their possessor to be truly great and good.

It is on this principle that we have endeavoured to proceed in analysing the many-sided character of the apostle Paul. In its general aspect, it stands out as that of an eminent preacher, a great sufferer, and a deeply exercised Christian. And in considering the features of his character in detail, we have seen that he was distinguished by unaffected *humility*, combined with high moral *dignity;* by transparent *unselfishness*, combined with strict *conscientiousness;* and by *large-heartedness*, combined with *tender-heartedness*. These qualities, viewed in combination, present to us one of the noblest ideals of human character that the world has ever seen, always excepting the unrivalled character of the Perfect Man, Christ Jesus, who is "altogether lovely," and the "chiefest among ten thousand." Eminent as Paul himself was in Christian grace and excellence, yet none felt more deeply than he did, how far short he came of that high standard of spotless virtue, and none laboured more strenuously than he to reach "the measure of the stature of the fulness of Christ." And this, let us never forget, must be the constant aim of every true Christian, viz., to become more like Christ, and to have the same mind that was in Him. Still, while He is to be our chief model, yet it will greatly assist us in our aspirations and efforts, to study the character of His most faithful followers, and to know how mightily His grace wrought in them, so that we may be encouraged and stimulated to "follow those who, through faith and patience, inherit the promises."

But our analysis of Paul's character would be very incomplete, without adverting to two additional features by which he was eminently distinguished, viz., his *intrepid courage, combined with habitual prayerfulness.* Both of these qualities are obviously essential to enable us to fight successfully the good fight of faith, and to exhibit in our daily conduct the reality and power of the Life of Faith. We need *courage* to resist and overcome the world, and the devil, and the flesh, in their various seductive forms of temptation; and we need *prayerfulness* to bring down to our help that Divine power and grace, without which we can do nothing. Every true Christian is most deeply sensible of his own utter weakness, and his total inability to discharge duty faithfully, to bear trial patiently, to encounter danger boldly, or to resist temptation successfully. But then he knows also where the needed strength is to be found; for he can say, Weak and helpless though I be in myself, yet "I CAN DO ALL THINGS THROUGH CHRIST WHO STRENGTHENETH ME."

I. INTREPID COURAGE.

When the apostle said, "I can do all things," this in his lips was not a mere empty boast, but it was a genuine expression of the whole tone and temper of his mind. From no duties, however difficult, and from no sacrifices, however painful, did he ever shrink, but as a true and brave soldier of Christ, he was ready to go anywhere, and to incur any hazard, and fight any battle, to which his marching orders called him. Great as his sufferings, and perils, and persecutions were, he met and bore them all, not only with unruffled tranquillity, but even with holy triumph. He was so elevated above the world by the principles he professed, that he seemed to move in a lofty region, where danger could not reach him, and fear could not disturb his mind; just as a man, on the summit of a lofty mountain, is raised far above the clouds, and can see the storm raging, and the lightning flashing far below, while he himself breathes a calm and pure atmosphere. Having committed the keeping of his soul to Christ, the apostle never had any apprehensions as to his personal safety; and being embarked in the noblest enterprise, and devoted to the service of the best of masters, he counted it a high honour to suffer shame for His sake. Dangers intensified his courage, and death had no terrors for him; but like Nehemiah, he could truly say, "Should such a man as I flee" from the post of duty and danger?

And all this is the more wonderful when we consider that Paul does not seem to have been remarkable for mere physical courage. With his sickly body and his sensitive spirit, it is evident, from the way in which he speaks of his sufferings, that he felt them most acutely, and that he naturally shrank from them, like any other man; as when he besought the Lord thrice to remove his "thorn in the flesh." His was not the brute courage of the war-horse which rushes impetuously into the thickest of the battle; nor the mere animal courage of the soldier, who is so carried away by the excitement of the combat, as to be insensible, for the time, to fear. But Paul's courage had no intermixture of rashness or fool-hardiness. He never courted persecution, or put himself needlessly in the way of danger; but when they could be honourably avoided, he never scrupled to do so. His intrepid courage was tempered with consummate prudence. It was *moral* courage of the noblest type, springing from a strong sense of duty to Christ, inspired by love and gratitude to Christ for His great salvation, and sustained by the promise and the power of that grace which rested upon him, and was made sufficient for him. There are two aspects in which his courage may be regarded.

First—*In resisting his enemies.* His boldness at Damascus has been already noticed. No sooner was he converted, than immediately (without losing a day), "he preached Christ in the synagogues, that He is the Son of God." In the face of obloquy and persecution, he "conferred not with flesh and blood;" but he publicly avowed the change that had been wrought upon him, and braved all consequences, rather than deny his Lord, of cease to proclaim the great salvation. Then after his three years' solitude in Arabia, he went up to Jerusalem; where "he spake *boldly* in the name of the Lord Jesus, and disputed against the Grecians: but they went about to slay him." Nor would he have left Jerusalem at all at this time, unless Jesus himself had appeared to him, as he was praying in the temple, and commanded him to make haste, and depart to the Gentiles (Acts xxii. 21). But so anxious was Paul to continue his labours there, and so convinced was he that his brethren would be sure to receive his testimony, that he ventured to remonstrate with his Lord, and entreated permission to remain in that den of murderers; and it was not till the command was repeated a second time, that he felt constrained to obey. What indomitable courage too did he exhibit amid the perils and persecutions which he endured in Asia Minor, as at Lystra and Ephesus; and subsequently in Europe, especially at Philippi; and how signally did he prove his readiness to endure hardships, "as a good soldier of Jesus Christ."

Secondly—Paul's moral courage appears *in opposing his friends*, when they were in the wrong. Here we do not refer merely to his stern denunciations of those pretended Christians, those Judaising teachers, who sought to undermine his influence, and who attempted to sow dissension in the churches, and to unsettle their faith, and corrupt their principles. To these men he would not yield subjection; no, not for an hour, nor even by a hair's breadth; but he plainly told them, "If any man preach any other Gospel unto you than that ye have received, let him be accursed." That was not the language of a time-server, or a popularity hunter: but it was the language of one, who had courage to follow the right at all hazards, and who, having the fear of God, was not troubled with any other fear.

But his moral courage appears still more conspicuously in his faithful dealing even with friends to whom he was warmly attached. When they fell into error and sin, he never hesitated to rebuke them sharply and yet lovingly. This is a far more difficult thing to do than to resist our avowed enemies. We all like to be on the best of terms with our friends, and we are prone to overlook their errors and faults, and to refrain from telling them our mind openly and frankly. The young are particularly liable to yield to this tendency. They are prone to sail with the stream, and to conform to the wishes and opinions and practices of their friends and companions; and they often lack courage to tell a brother his faults, and to warn him of their consequences, when truth demands plain speaking and stern reproof. But Paul was of a totally different stamp. Those whom he loved best he reproved the most severely, when their conduct deserved it. Thus, when the Galatian church was corrupted by false teaching, and seduced from the simplicity of faith, he faithfully reproved them, saying, "Am I therefore become your enemy because I tell you the truth?" Even with his beloved friend Barnabas he had a "sharp contention," because the latter desired to take his nephew, Mark, with him on their missionary journey, after the young man had abandoned the work of the Lord for a time. But Paul was resolved to teach the young missionary a useful lesson, and to make him feel that he could only regain lost confidence by steady and consistent conduct; and therefore he denied even the earnest request of Barnabas, who had been such a warm friend to himself; and "the contention was so sharp between them, that they departed asunder, the one from the other." Still, there was no ill-will or grudge in Paul's mind, for when afterwards Mark proved himself worthy to be trusted, he became one of the apostle's most cherished friends; as he tells us, in writing to Timothy from Rome, a short time before his martyrdom, "Take Mark, and bring him with thee, for he is profitable to me for the ministry."

Another proof of Paul's fearless courage was given at Antioch, when he withstood his fellow-apostle Peter "to the face, because he was to be blamed" for giving countenance by his conduct to the false doctrine that the observance of the ceremonial law ought to be imposed upon the Gentiles as needful to salvation. It must have been a sore trial to him to be compelled to rebuke, before the whole church, one whom he so highly esteemed as a "pillar" in the house of God. But his fidelity and courage caused no estrangement between them, for Peter speaks subsequently of his "beloved brother Paul," and of the "wisdom given unto him." Good men may differ in opinion; but if they are really good men, their love will be without dissimulation, and their rebukes will be without bitterness or enmity; and they will be ready to say, "Let the righteous smite me, it shall be a kindness; and let him reprove me, it shall be an excellent oil, which shall not break my head," but which shall heal wounds and soften asperity.

From all this it is evident that Paul was not a man of compromise or lax principle in any question of vital importance, but that he was bold and fearless in standing up for the truth as it is in Jesus. None was more yielding and accommodating in matters of indifference; but none was more firm and inflexible than he in the great questions of Christian doctrine and duty—such questions as that of justification by faith alone, and that of the necessity of personal sanctification.

Now, such courage as this must appear very remarkable to any one who is capable of appreciating it. We cannot but admire the courage of a skilful and brave general on the field of battle when he puts his enemies to flight; but how little could he do if he stood *alone*, and if he were not backed by the ardour and enthusiasm of his faithful and valiant troops! And yet Paul stood in a great measure alone, in that life-long conflict which he waged with human passions and with the rulers of this world, and with spiritual wickedness in high places. In his most trying and difficult positions he had occasion to say, "At my first answer" (before Nero) "no man stood with me, but all men forsook me: I pray God that it may not be laid to their charge. Notwithstanding, the Lord stood with me, and strengthened me." Therefore even when alone, and destitute of all human help, his courage never failed and his resolution never faltered; and at length his struggles were crowned with victory and his labours with success. And the source of all his courage was his simple faith in Christ, and his realising sense of his Master's gracious presence with him. Having hold of Christ's almighty arm, he was held up amid all his trials and temptations, and was made strong in his conscious weakness; and therefore he could truly say, "I can do all things through Christ who strengtheneth me."

A few years ago, when our country was supposed to be threatened with an invasion from France, thousands of our young men, influenced by loyalty and patriotism, volunteered their services in defence of our homes and altars; and their noble deed averted the threatened evil, and secured for us the blessings of peace. But there is a still nobler warfare, which the Captain of salvation summons them to wage. What is living Christianity but a constant war with evil, without and within—a war of defence against sin and Satan, and a war that is waged with the view of ultimate peace? It is called a "great fight of afflictions," and the "good fight of faith," and a "wrestling," not only with flesh and blood, but also with "principalities and powers." To secure the victory, we must be "clothed with the whole armour of God," with the breastplate of righteousness, the shield of faith, and the "sword of the Spirit, which is the Word of God." There is no exemption, and no "discharge in that war" with evil, so long as we remain on earth, for either we must overcome sin, or sin will overcome us; and if we refuse to fight along with Christ, we must perish along with Satan. Should it not, then, be the highest ambition of every young man, not only to enlist under the banner of the Cross, but also to prove, by his strenuous resistance to sin, by fidelity to the great Captain, and by deeds of Christian valour, that he is not only a soldier, but a "*good* soldier of Jesus Christ?"

The first duty of a soldier is to give implicit obedience to the orders of his chief. He must not please himself, nor follow his own inclination, but he must be ready to obey his general, in the face of danger and death. His motto must be to do or die. So the Christian must obey his "marching orders;" and his constant inquiry must be, "Lord, what wilt thou have me to do?" and having learned from His written instructions in the Bible what the will of the Lord is, his simple duty is to obey without question or cavil. Then he must be ready to "endure hardness" in the Master's service, to encounter difficulties fearlessly, to bear trials patiently, and to resist temptations courageously. He is engaged in a life-and-death struggle, with corruption within, with an ungodly world without, and with the wicked one both within and without; and the only alternative is defeat or victory.

Taking Paul, then, as his model, let every young man aim at being a *good* soldier of Christ. What are the qualifications of a "good soldier?" One is that he must not be a craven or coward, who flees from the battle or yields to the foe, but a man of true courage, of unquestionable valour, and unshrinking resolution in contending for the right. Such was the apostle Paul, and such must we be, and such shall we be if we know the power of a living Christianity.

Another qualification of a "good soldier" is love to his general, combined with confidence in his military skill. We are told that the first Napoleon had a singular power of winning the affections of his armies, and that this was the grand secret of his wonderful success. "Cut deeper," said a dying soldier to the surgeon when extracting a ball from his breast,—"cut deeper, and you will find the Emperor in my heart." So every true Christian has Christ dwelling in his heart, as the object of his supreme love; and true love makes all his labour light, and all his service pleasant, and all his fighting easy.

Another qualification of a good soldier is readiness for active service. "No man that warreth," says Paul, "entangleth himself with the affairs of this life, that he may please Him who hath chosen him to be a soldier." Instead of allowing his mind and energy to be frittered away with frivolous and alien pursuits, with self-indulgence or engrossing worldly business, the Christian must be ever on the watch, and mind the one business for which he was placed in the ranks, and be always *ready* to do and to dare whatever his great Captain prescribes to him. Such was the readiness of Lord Clyde, to go forth on a day's notice to India to quell the mutiny, and rescue our besieged soldiers in Lucknow; and the readiness also of the apostolic William Burns, when, on being appointed to go as a missionary to China, and being asked when he would be ready, he said, "To-morrow." And so, without bidding farewell to his parents, he immediately embarked, landed in China, and did a great and good work there, and thus proved himself to be a "good soldier of Jesus Christ." Let young men therefore do likewise. Let them be strong and of a good courage in the service of the best of masters; and instead of being "entangled with the affairs of this life," with its pleasures or business, let them mind the one great business of life, which is to conquer sin in their own hearts, to do all the good they can, to prepare for a holy heaven, and bring as many as possible along with them to that better land. Thus, being always ready for active service, they will manifest the power of a living Christianity. And when their hearts are ready to faint, let them be encouraged by the thought that the victory has been won for them by the great Captain, and that He has promised abundant grace to help them, and has given the prospect of a crown of glory which fadeth not away.

II. HABITUAL PRAYERFULNESS.

Many are courageous from mere self-reliance, and their boldness has little or no element of dependence on God. They plan and propose to do this or that, in utter forgetfulness that it is God who disposes, and that without Him they can do nothing. Their language is, "By the strength of my hand I have done it, and by my wisdom; for I am prudent." But Paul's heroic courage was as far as possible removed from self-confidence. Bold and fearless though he was, yet he was also deeply humble and habitually prayerful. Though, like our own great Reformer, he "never feared the face of man;" yet the reason of this was that he feared God, and depended implicitly upon Him for every good thought, and design, and deed. "Not," he said, "as though we were sufficient of ourselves to think anything as of ourselves, but our sufficiency is of God." This was the real secret of his strength, and the true source of his courage, and of all those other graces which adorned his character. His life throughout was not one of self-reliance, but of conscious weakness and constant dependence on Christ. His prevailing sentiments were, "I am crucified with Christ: nevertheless I live; yet not I, but Christ liveth in me: and the life which I now live in the flesh I live by the faith of the Son of God, who loved me, and gave Himself for me." He never for a moment imagined that he could do anything of himself, either in the way of subduing the evil in his own heart, or of benefiting his fellow-men, or of advancing in the divine life, or of glorifying his Master; but all his services and attainments he ascribed entirely to that grace of God which was given to him in answer to prayer. "I can do all things," not of myself or by my own power, but only "*through Christ who strengtheneth me.*"

In tracing his Christian experience, it is very evident that he was habitually given to prayer. One of his first utterances after his conversion was a prayer for Divine guidance—"Lord, what wilt Thou have me to do?" Then, during the three days of his blindness and soul conflict at Damascus, described in Rom. vii. 7-12, he was so wholly given to earnest supplication, that this was told to Ananias as the evidence of his conversion—"Behold, he prayeth." Often before, he had said "long prayers," like the Pharisees, but never till now had he really prayed from his heart, as a sinner thirsting for salvation. This prayerfulness was the key-note of all his subsequent career; and his whole history, as recorded in the Acts and in his own epistles, shows that he lived and moved in an atmosphere of prayer. It was such a marked feature in his character, that it is needless to specify instances. It may be noticed, however, that almost every prayer he offered up for blessings desired was blended with thanksgivings for blessings bestowed. He not only "continued in prayer," but he "watched in the same with thanksgiving." He did not pray as one who beat the air, and who had no hope of success, but as one who expected and obtained answers, to furnish matter of praise. The union of prayer with thanksgiving appears in many of his addresses, both to individuals and to churches, a few examples of which may be seen in Phile. 4-6; 2 Tim. i. 3-4; Rom. i. 8-11; Phil. i. 3-6; Col. i. 3-6.

All this evidently shows that Paul combined, with his intrepid courage, a spirit of true devotion, and that he spent much of his time in secret prayer, and personal communion with God; and that he regarded this not only as an incumbent duty, but as a most precious and profitable privilege. In all this, the apostle closely resembled his Divine Master, who spent whole nights in prayer on the mountain top. So Paul prayed "*night and day*" for that Divine strength which he felt that he so greatly needed to uphold him, and to render his labours successful. Nor was his prayer a mere cry of distress or a groan of anguish; but its union with thanksgiving shows that it was a prayer of faith, which was graciously answered. Prayer granted gave him ground of praise; and praise for mercies received led to renewed prayer for more. Thus his religion was not a gloomy but a gladsome religion; far removed from that of the monk's cloister or the hermit's cell, and making his heart glad with the sunshine of God's reconciled countenance, and the peace of a good conscience, and the hope of eternal bliss.

Here, then, is a model for young men. With moral courage in resisting evil and standing up boldly for truth, let them combine habitual prayerfulness, for this is the very life of the soul—the secret of its power and the source of its comfort and joy. To live without prayer is to live without God, and without hope in the world. In restraining or neglecting prayer we can neither be furnished for our present duty nor fitted for our future destiny. As prayer is essential in the beginning of the work of grace, so it is no less essential to the subsequent progress and the ultimate completion of that work. Prayer brings down to our help the mighty power of God. It is that master-key which unlocks the treasury of heaven's grace. It is that electric chain which, piercing the skies, sends flashes of celestial light into the dark soul, and refreshes God's weary heritage with copious showers of blessing. It is mighty through God, for it moves the hand which moves the world; and there is no mountain of guilt which it cannot throw down, no corruption which it cannot subdue, no sorrow which it cannot soothe, and no spiritual blessing which it cannot secure. "Verily, verily," says Christ, "whatsoever ye shall ask the Father in my name, He will give it you." If, then, we desire to be freed from the burden of sin, or to bear patiently the trials of life, or to overcome its temptations, or to surmount its difficulties and dangers, we must let our requests be made known to God; and then, receiving power from on high, we shall be enabled boldly to say, like Paul, "I can do all things through Christ who strengtheneth me."

And let us learn from this subject the great lesson, that our salvation, though impossible with men, is possible with God. No doubt there are great obstacles in the way, and the greatest of them are to be found in ourselves; in our pride of heart, in our self-righteousness, and in our love of sin; and these we have no power to overcome. We cannot subdue our pride, so as to make ourselves willing to be saved by free and sovereign grace. Neither can we renounce our self-righteousness, so as to constrain us to rely on Christ's righteousness alone for our justification. Nor can we overcome our inveterate love of sin, so as to devote our hearts and lives to the service and glory of God; but all these things we shall be able easily to do "through Christ strengthening us." Let no one say, as the apostles once said, when they were told of the difficulty of a rich man entering into the kingdom of God, "Who then can be saved?" For Christ says, Every one who comes to me shall be saved. And if you ask, How *can* I come, for I am weak and helpless? the answer is, You *can* come, through the power of the promised Spirit, who is given to all that ask Him. Great as the difficulties are (and the more that we face them and realise them so much the better), still, "is anything too hard for the Lord?" If any man really wishes to be saved, let him offer up in sincerity such a prayer as this: "O Lord, I cannot save myself, but Thou canst do it, and Thou hast said that Thou art most willing to do it, by the blood of atonement and by the baptism of the Holy Ghost and of fire. Lord, I believe, help Thou mine unbelief; draw me, and I will run after Thee; turn me, and I shall be turned; save me, and I shall be saved."

In our next chapter we shall speak of "Paul the aged," and the continued evidence which he gave, in the closing years of his life, of his possession of those graces by which, as we have seen, he was so eminently distinguished. "They shall still bring forth fruit in old age."

CHAPTER VI.

GROWTH IN GRACE.

"Paul the aged, and now also a prisoner of Jesus Christ."
—Phile. 9.

WE have endeavoured to analyse the character of Paul, and to present in combination its more prominent features, as these are exhibited incidentally in his own epistles, and partly, also, in the history of his life, contained in the Acts of the Apostles. That history, however, terminates about five years before his martyrdom in the year 68; and we naturally wish to know, not only what he said and did afterwards, but also whether he maintained the same high character to the close of his life. Not a few who have long borne a Christian character have subsequently fallen away. Having put their hand to the plough, they looked back, and drew back;—having apparently begun the Christian race, they stopped short and missed the prize. Was Paul then one of these? Did his faith fail, and his love wax cold, and his zeal decay, in the winter of old age?

Or did he realise the beautiful description of the Psalmist, " The righteous shall flourish like the palm tree ; they shall still bring forth fruit in old age?"

The answer to these questions we hope to furnish in this and a subsequent chapter. But have we any reliable materials to enable us to do so? There are many to whom his history, after his first imprisonment in Rome, is almost an utter blank; and there are others whose knowledge of it is very imperfect and confused; and yet that history, though not recorded in the Acts of the Apostles, is, in some respects, the most interesting and instructive chapter in his eventful life. It shows us that, amid the growing infirmities of old age, and the rigours and solitude of imprisonment, and in the immediate prospect of a bloody death, he " held fast the beginning of his confidence, steadfast unto the end." It shows that his gracious Master did not forsake him, when his heart and flesh were fainting and failing; but that, through abounding grace, his Christian excellences shone with increasing splendour, and that, like the sun, he was most glorious at his setting.

We propose, therefore, to endeavour to fill up the gap in his history between the years 63 and 68; and the materials, for enabling us to do so, are to be found in those of his own epistles which were written during that period. On this subject, much light has been thrown by Paley in his " Horæ Paulinæ," in which a very impressive argument, in favour of the authenticity of Scripture, has been drawn from the undesigned coincidences between the historical statements of Luke, and the casual allusions made to them in Paul's own writings. More recently, a valuable contribution to the elucidation of the "Life and Epistles of St Paul," has been made by the admirable work of Conybeare and Howson.

Such, then, are some of the sources from which we have to draw the materials of our present chapter; in which we shall have occasion to refer to the apostle's position and occupation during his first imprisonment at Rome, in the years 63 and 64. In these painful circumstances, instead of being idle, fretful, or desponding, he was active, energetic, and hopeful. Though he expected no mercy at the hands of the cruel tyrant before whom he was to be brought, yet he diligently improved every opportunity afforded to him, of preaching the Gospel, and of sending precious letters to the churches which he had planted, and which were now beyond the reach of his voice. His enforced leisure was employed in winning souls to Christ, and confirming those who had already believed. He reminds us of Luther when, at a critical period in the history of the Reformation, he was snatched from his persecutors and shut up in the Castle of the Wartburg, where his leisure was employed in translating the Word of God for the benefit of the common people, and in sending forth his withering exposures of the papal Antichrist. So Paul, on whom devolved the "care of all the churches," was not prevented by his growing infirmities, or his imminent danger, from doing his Master's work with all his might. In him, young men may see what they might do for Christ in the most adverse circumstances; and they may also learn, that if they give themselves to Christ in their youth, as Paul did, He will not forsake them in old age, but will make their latter end better and happier than their beginning.

When the apostle was brought to Rome, he was handed over by Julius, the centurion, to the commander of the imperial guard. Instead, however, of being shut up in the common prison, he was allowed to reside in the house of one of his Christian friends, probably that of Aquila and Priscilla. Considerable liberty, therefore, was at this time granted to him, and the only restraint that he was subjected to was, that he was chained by his right arm to a Roman soldier. All his friends had free access to him, and many inquirers came to him to be taught the way of salvation. Thus the Gospel came to be well known in Rome, and even in the imperial palace itself; and many converts to the Christian faith were to be found in "Cæsar's household," as we shall afterwards see. So great was the concourse of inquirers that the accommodation of his "lodging" became inadequate, and he was obliged to rent a house of his own, where "he dwelt two whole years, and received all that came in unto him."

It was not, therefore, till about the close of these two years, that the appeal, which Paul had taken to the emperor at Cæsarea, was heard and ultimately sustained. This delay was probably caused by the circumstance, that his accusers were long in reaching Rome, so that the trial could not proceed without them; and no doubt their arrival might be delayed by their laborious efforts to collect evidence of Paul's alleged seditious tendencies, and to bring witnesses in support of their various charges against him. Besides, the proceedings in the Roman courts were often very dilatory, especially when the accused was tried on more charges than one, because it was the custom to pronounce sentence upon the first charge, before the second was entered upon.

How then was Paul occupied during these two years? One occupation, as Luke informs us, was daily preaching, often "from morning till evening." He "preached the kingdom of God, and taught those things which concern the Lord Jesus Christ, with all confidence." And how impressive and touching must have been the glowing eloquence of that "ambassador in bonds!" What force would be given to his arguments, and what pathos to his appeals, when he raised his chained hand to implore sinners, in Christ's stead, to be reconciled to God! and when the harsh clank-

Fruit in Old Age. 99

ing of his chain accompanied the sound of his solemn and persuasive voice, who could doubt his thorough sincerity, or fail to admire his high moral courage, and his burning zeal for the honour of Christ, and for the salvation of his fellow-men?

But besides daily preaching during these two years, his time was also much occupied with the care of all the churches. To some of them he had already written various epistles, such as those to the Thessalonians about the year 54, and that to the Galatians about the year 58, and those to the Corinthians about the years 59 and 60, and that to the Romans about the year 60. These are all which he had yet written, and it was necessary now to write the Acts of the Apostles, which was done by Luke under Paul's direction, and also various other epistles, which were soon to form part of the inspired record.

To these, therefore, let us now direct our attention, not for the purpose of expounding them fully, but simply for the purpose of bringing out the incidental notices which they give us of Paul's personal history, and of the state of his mind in the prospect of a sentence of death at Cæsar's tribunal. It will be interesting also to observe who were his companions and fellow-labourers at this time in Rome.

(1.) Of these epistles, the first was that addressed to Philemon, which seems to have been written about a year after Paul's arrival, that is in the year 64. From the salutation in the last verse, it appears that Timothy, his beloved son in the faith, was now at his side to cheer him with his sympathy, and to help him in the work of the Lord. Philemon was a man of high social position at Colosse, and a member of the Christian church which Paul had planted there. He was one of the fruits of Paul's apostolic labours, having been brought through his instrumentality to a saving knowledge of the truth. This Philemon had a slave called Onesimus, who had robbed his master, and run away from his house, and fled to Rome. Wandering about the streets there, Onesimus was brought by some means within the reach of Paul's influence, and was converted to the Christian faith; for he calls him "my son Onesimus, whom I have begotten in my bonds." When this runaway slave was converted, he gave such evidence of superior gifts and grace, that Paul would gladly have retained him at Rome, and employed him in the service of the Gospel. But he would do nothing without the leave of his master Philemon, and therefore he wrote to him beseeching him to forgive his robbery and flight, and to receive him now, not as a slave, but as a "brother beloved." From this brief epistle, so remarkable for its tact and politeness and Christian feeling, we see how living Christianity operates upon the relation of master and slave. It seeks to emancipate the slave, not by violent means or bloody wars, but by leavening society with the holy and benevolent spirit of that Gospel, which proclaims the equality of all men in the sight of God, and which denounces every attempt to deprive a brother of his liberty. In this epistle there is a happy blending of Christian wisdom with Christian tenderness.

(2.) The second of the epistles, written at this time, is that addressed to the *Colossians*, a church of Phrygia in Asia Minor. This district had been visited by Paul on two different occasions (Acts xvi. 6, xviii. 23), although it is not expressly stated that, on either, he had visited the town of Colosse. Probably the church there was founded by Epaphras, who was at this time in Rome with the apostle; for he says (i. 7) that they had learned the Gospel " of Epaphras, our dear fellow-servant, who is for you a faithful minister of Christ." Then, this epistle was sent to the Colossians by Tychicus, whom he calls "a beloved brother and a faithful minister" (iv. 7-9). Paul's object, in writing this epistle, was to warn the Colossians against various errors and sinful practices, into which they had fallen, especially the errors of a false philosophy, and the worship of angels, and certain Judaising customs. In opposition to these, he inculcates upon them the simple truth of the Gospel, and the pure morality of the Christian life. From the conclusion of the epistle, we learn that Paul's fellow-labourers at this time, besides Timothy, Tychicus, and

Epaphras, were Aristarchus, the companion of his voyage and shipwreck, and Mark, whom he had formerly distrusted, but to whom he was now reconciled, and Justus; also Luke, the beloved physician and inspired historian, and Demas, who as yet was faithful, but who afterwards "forsook him, having loved this present world" (iv. 10-14). It is peculiarly interesting to read these notices of that small but devoted missionary band, who were now grappling, in the strength of the Lord of Hosts, with the idolatry and profligacy of imperial Rome; and whose doctrines, though proclaimed by humble prisoners, were destined to overthrow the empire of the Cæsars, and to revolutionise the world. At the head of this band, Paul himself stood, strong in faith and undaunted in spirit, and full of confidence in the ultimate triumph of the Gospel over all opposition.

(3.) The third of the epistles, written at this time, was that to the church of Ephesus, the chief of the seven churches of Asia. In this epistle, which was sent by Tychicus, at the same time as the former (vi. 21, 22), Paul sets forth, in glowing language, the high privileges which the Gospel had conferred upon the Gentiles, and their consequent obligation to walk worthy of these privileges, and to adorn their Christian profession by a holy life and conversation.

(4.) But there was a fourth epistle, written shortly after this time, viz., that to the Philippians: and it demands our special notice on account of the numerous allusions which it contains to Paul's state, and feelings, and prospects, during his first imprisonment at Rome.

It is very evident that the apostle cherished a peculiarly strong affection for his converts at Philippi, while their reciprocal affection for him, as their spiritual father, was scarcely less strong. The Philippian church was the first-fruits of his labours in Europe; and it included the converted jailer and his family, and also Lydia, whose heart the Lord opened, and who entertained him hospitably in her house. And though the members of that church were generally poor in outward estate, yet they were distinguished, more perhaps than those of any other, by their large-hearted liberality, especially in ministering repeatedly to the apostle's temporal wants. Previous to this time, they had on various occasions sent liberal contributions for his support; and as soon as they heard of his imprisonment at Rome, they resolved to send a special messenger there, to declare their heartfelt sympathy with him in his affliction, and to give tangible proof of it by ministering to the necessities of their beloved teacher. That messenger was Epaphroditus, who seems to have been a leading presbyter in the Philippian church, and who cheerfully undertook this long voyage to Rome at the call of that church (ii. 25, 30). It appears, however, that he had been exposed to great danger on the way, and had risked his life to render this service to the apostle. It was by him also, that Paul sent the epistle to the Philippians, soon after the other three already mentioned, about the year 64 or 65. It is touching to observe how grateful Paul was for their considerate kindness, and how highly he appreciated their spontaneous gifts (read chap. iv. 10-19).

In this affectionate epistle, we have several very interesting and suggestive notices of the *results* of Paul's labours in Rome, showing his unabated zeal and untiring assiduity in his Master's service, as, for instance, in chap. i., verses 12-14. From these verses it appears that his patience and courage as an "ambassador in bonds," and as one expecting to be tried for his life, had tended greatly to the furtherance of the Gospel, and had emboldened even the timid to speak the Word fearlessly. Even in the "palace" itself, that is, in the *prætorium*, the residence of the imperial guard, his case was well known, and his preaching had produced a powerful effect. The *prætorium* was situated in the very centre of the city, on that Palatine Hill which was "at once the birthplace of the infant city, and the abode of its rulers during its days of greatest splendour, where the reed-thatched cottage of Romulus was still preserved in the midst of the gorgeous structures of Caligula and Nero." It was there that the Emperor Augustus was born, and this hill was at that time "the most conspicuous spot on the earth, not merely for crime, but for splendour and power." And yet even there, among the imperial guards of Nero, the preaching of the apostle was "the power of God unto salvation." Nay, in the household of Nero himself, not a few converts to the faith were to be found; for at the close of the epistle, the apostle says, "All the saints salute you, chiefly *they that are of Cæsar's household.*"

Still further, we learn from this epistle that Paul's position had now become far more critical, and that his prospect of being set at liberty was growing darker. To this he refers in chap. ii., verses 17-23. One reason probably why he apprehended an unfavourable result, in his approaching trial, was the marriage of Nero about this time to the infamous Poppæa, who had become a proselyte to Judaism, and whose influence with the emperor would certainly be employed in favour of Paul's accusers. This abandoned woman had persuaded Nero, not only to divorce his young wife Octavia, but also to put her to death. Her impiety was so flagrant that when she gave birth to a daughter, she had temples erected to herself and her infant, and divine honours paid to them both. We are told by Josephus that she employed her influence with Nero in favour of the Jews; and no doubt it would be exerted against Paul, when brought before the emperor's judgment-seat.

And yet, in these circumstances of distress and danger, the apostle possessed his soul in patience, and prosecuted his labours with unabated activity and uninterrupted success. Even the rough soldiers, who guarded him, were struck with amazement in witnessing his calm self-possession, his heroic courage, and his untiring diligence in preaching the Gospel of the grace of God. While their profligate master was running a career of almost unexampled wickedness, and fast filling up the measure of his iniquity, yet not a few of his servants were persuaded to renounce their idols and their vices, and to become good soldiers of Jesus Christ.

It has been justly remarked that "history has few stranger contrasts than that, on the one hand, of the impious and profligate Nero seated on the throne of the Cæsars, and satiating his lust and cruelty without fear or restraint; and on the other hand, that of Paul the prisoner, chained in Nero's *prætorium*, keeping his body in subjection, calmly waiting his impending sentence, and labouring all day long to proclaim the glad tidings of salvation to all who would come to his house." At this time, "there were but two religions in the Roman world; the worship of the emperor, and the worship of the Saviour. The old superstitions had been long worn out; they had lost all hold on educated minds. There remained, to civilised heathens, no other worship possible but the worship of power; and the incarnation of power which they chose was, very naturally, the sovereign of the world. These, then, were the ultimate results of the noble intuitions of Plato, the methodical reasoning of Aristotle, the pure morality of Socrates. All had failed for want of external sanction and Divine authority. There was left nothing but the sensual philosophy of Epicurus, and the debasing religion of Nero-worship. But a new doctrine had now been taught in Rome, and was believed even on the Palatine Hill. Over against the altars of Nero and Poppæa, the voice of a prisoner was daily heard for two whole years, and daily woke up in dead souls the consciousness of their Divine origin, and of their high duty and destiny as immortal beings. Men listened to him, and learned the way of salvation; and they came to know that self-sacrifice was better than self-indulgence, and that to suffer was nobler than to reign. They felt that the only religion which satisfied the needs of man was the religion of godly sorrow, the religion of self-devotion, the *religion of the cross*" ("Life and Epistles of St Paul," p. 533).

This lesson the world still needs to learn. Even yet, in the full blaze of Gospel light, there is a strong tendency in many minds to walk in the sparks of their own kindling, and to revive the exploded philosophies of ancient times. Men, professing themselves to be wise, have become fools. How humbling to find, in this nineteenth century, that men of high scientific attainments, in endeavouring to explain the creation of the world, and deny its Creator, have dragged forth from its grave the theory of a heathen philosopher, and ascribed the origin of all things to a "fortuitous concourse of atoms." Modern science and philosophy are set up as far superior to God's revelation of His will, and far better suited to an age of progress and mental development. Many are losing their hold of Gospel truth, and are tossed on a sea of uncertainty as to its simplest principles. It has been truly remarked that this backward tendency "might well surprise us did we not know that the progress of human reason, in the path of ethical or moral discovery, is merely the progress of a man in a treadmill, doomed for ever to retrace his own steps." True progress can only be realised by holding fast the truth as it is in Jesus, and taking His Word as a lamp to our feet and a light to our path. The Gospel which Paul preached has lost none of its power in the lapse of ages. It is the "everlasting Gospel," which shall yet be preached to all nations, and by which all nations shall yet be blessed. It is still as much suited to man's deepest wants, as it was in the days of Paul, and it is mighty, through God, in casting down the strongholds of sin and Satan in the human heart, and in bringing all its thoughts and affections into captivity to the obedience of Christ.

Let young men, therefore, prize this glorious Gospel, and never be ashamed of its precious and saving truths. Let them beware of being led away by prevailing errors, and of substituting the dim light of human reason for the clear and blessed light of revelation. Paul was not ashamed of the Gospel, and why? "Because it is the power of God unto salvation to every one that believeth; to the Jew first, and also to the Greek." Let every young man embrace the Gospel with his whole heart for his personal salvation, and let him strive to maintain a life and conversation becoming the Gospel, and thus exhibit, in all his actings, the practical power of a living Christianity. And in imitation of the apostolic zeal and fervent devotedness of Paul, let all strive to diffuse the Gospel by works of faith and deeds of self-denial; and hasten the time when Christ's parting charge to his Church shall be fulfilled: "Preach the Gospel to every creature; and lo! I am with you alway, even unto the end of the world."

In the next chapter, we shall refer to the labours of the apostle in the three closing years of his life, and to his martyrdom at Rome.

CHAPTER VII.

THE NEAR PROSPECT OF DEATH.

"I am now ready to be offered, and the time of my departure is at hand. I have fought a good fight, I have finished my course, I have kept the faith: henceforth there is laid up for me a crown of righteousness."—2 TIM. iv. 6-8.

IT has been truly said that "as a man lives, so he dies." If during life he walks by faith, we may be sure that he will die in faith. Or if he lives in sin and unbelief, it is but too probable that he will die without God, and without hope. The grace of God no doubt is omnipotent, and it can save to the uttermost, and even at the latest hour of existence. But a deathbed repentance is a rare occurrence. There is only one instance of it recorded in Scripture—that of the thief upon the cross; and while it teaches us that none should despair, it also teaches us that none should presume, or reckon too confidently on receiving at last that Divine mercy, which had been repeatedly offered, and as often refused. *Now* is the only " accepted time " that we can count upon ; " now is the day of salvation." We must become righteous, and must live the life of the righteous, if we desire to have a sure hope that our "latter end will be like his." This is one great lesson which the life of the apostle Paul teaches us. For about thirty years he had now been an eminent, faithful, and devoted servant of Christ; and his Master did not forsake him in old age, or in the near prospect of death. While his outward man decayed, the inward man was renewed day by day. "The righteous shall flourish like the palm-tree: he shall grow like a cedar in Lebanon. Those that be planted in the house of the Lord shall flourish in the courts of our God. They shall *still bring forth fruit in old age;* they shall be fat and flourishing; to show that the Lord is upright." The truth of all this, with reference to the great apostle, it will be our object to show in the present chapter, in order that young men may learn the advantage of early piety, and the blessedness of early consecration to Him who says, "I will never leave thee, nor forsake thee."

In endeavouring to trace the life and labours of the apostle Paul, we have now reached the close of his first imprisonment and trial at Rome. This, it is generally thought, took place about the year 64 or 65 of the Christian era; and seeing that he was put to death in the year that Nero died, that is in the year 68, there still remained for him three or four years of active labour in the service of his Divine Lord. It may not, therefore, be uninteresting or uninstructive, to endeavour to trace his course during that period, in so far as it is possible to do so. But as to this part of his history, the "Acts of the Apostles" are silent; and the notices given of his subsequent labours, even in his own epistles, are very brief and fragmentary. Still, by comparing one passage with another, as has been done so well by Paley in his "Horæ Paulinæ," and by Conybeare and Howson, we may obtain a tolerably correct idea of the apostle's spirit, and manner of life, during these closing years, and of his hopes and prospects at the hour of death. In giving us these fragmentary notices, instead of a detailed history, there was evidently a wise Providential design. For, as has been truly said, "the wall of separation, which for ever cuts off the apostolic age from that which followed it, was built by God. That age of miracles was not to be revealed to us as passing, by any gradual transition, into the common life of the Church; but it was intentionally isolated from all succeeding time, that we might learn to appreciate more fully its extraordinary character, and see by the sharpness of the abruptest contrast, the difference between the Divine and the human."

It is necessary, however, first to advert to the grounds on which we have reason to believe that Paul lived and laboured for at least three years after the close of his first imprisonment. One of these grounds is, that there are various allusions made in his subsequent epistles to his personal history, which can only be explained on this supposition. Then, too, it was the universal belief of the ancient Church that his appeal to Cæsar was sustained, that he was acquitted of the charges preferred against him in Judæa, and that he spent several years in active labour before he was again imprisoned and put to death. As to this, there is one emphatic testimony borne by a very competent witness, viz., Clement, one of his own disciples and fellow-labourers, of whom Paul says that "his name was in the book of life" (Phil. iv. 3). This Clement was a resident at Rome after the death of the apostle, and in an epistle of his, which is still extant, he says, " Paul, having been a herald" (of the Gospel) "in the east and *in the west*, enjoyed the distinguished celebrity due to his faith; and having taught righteousness to the whole world" (that is, the Roman empire), " even *to the furthest extremity of the west*, and having testified before princes, he thus departed from the world." This expression—" the furthest extremity of the west"—as used by an inhabitant of Rome, could only mean the western part of Europe, probably Spain. We know that Paul had long cherished a desire to preach the Gospel in that country, and that he had resolved to go there as soon as he should visit Rome; for in his Epistle to the Romans (xv. 23, 24), he says, "Now having no more place in these parts, and having a great desire these many years to come unto you; whensoever I take *my journey into Spain*, I will come to you." And to show how much his heart was set upon this, he adds (verse 28), "I *will come by you*" (Romans) "*into Spain.*" Many similar testimonies, by Christian writers of a later date, such as Eusebius and Chrysostom, might be adduced to show that Paul, after his release, went forth again to preach the Gospel and visit the churches, and that he reached Spain, and came back a second time to Rome, and that there he suffered a martyr's death, under the reign of the Emperor Nero.

In order to fill up this gap in Paul's history, and show how he was occupied during the closing years of his life, there are three things to be considered, viz.—his first trial and release at Rome, his subsequent labours, and his second trial and martyrdom.

I. His First Trial and Release at Rome.

This trial, as we have said, came on about the year 65, before the emperor himself, who was assisted by a council of twenty assessors, including the two consuls and a number of senators, and others of the highest rank. Such trials before the emperor were conducted in the imperial palace, which stood on the Palatine Hill, and the ruins of which are still to be seen there. At such a tribunal, the most august in the world, the apostle could expect little justice and less mercy;

though doubtless he rejoiced in the opportunity of proclaiming, before such an audience, the unsearchable riches of Christ. The power of life and death was in the hands of an unprincipled profligate and cruel despot, whose character and crimes were a disgrace to the lowest type of humanity. But Paul knew well that *his life* was not in the hands of Nero; and that he could suffer no injury so long as his Master had anything for him to do in this world. "The servant of God is immortal till his work is done." Nor had Paul any fear of death; but he was quite willing and ready to "depart and be with Christ, which is far better." What his feelings were, in the prospect of appearing before Cæsar to be tried for his life, we may learn from the epistle which he had just sent away to the Philippians by Epaphroditus. There he says, "To me to live is Christ, and to die is gain. But if I live in the flesh, this is the fruit of my labour: yet what I shall choose I wot not. For I am in a strait betwixt two, having a desire to depart, and to be with Christ; which is far better: nevertheless to abide in the flesh is more needful for you. And having this confidence, I know that I shall abide and continue with you all, for your furtherance and joy of faith" (Phil. i. 21-25). From this we see that his mind was uncertain, not only as to what his sentence would be, but also as to whether he ought to desire to remain on earth, or to depart to his eternal rest above. But whatever the result might be, he possessed his soul in patience and submission to the Divine will.

Now, though we have no formal account of this important trial, yet we know what was the nature of the charges preferred against the apostle. They were these—sedition, heresy, and sacrilege. To prove these against him, his Jewish prosecutors again appeared at Cæsar's judgment-seat, as they had done at the tribunal of Felix and Festus before; and they endeavoured to show that Paul was guilty of these crimes, and worthy of death. And we can also conceive what the line of Paul's defence would be in proving his innocence; and no doubt he would electrify that august audience, as he had done before those who heard him at Cæsarea in the presence of King Agrippa, by his simple statement of the facts of the case, by his powerful arguments, and by his eloquent appeals to his just rights as a Roman citizen. As to that charge, which would be regarded at Rome as the most serious of all—viz., sedition—he would be able to show conclusively that, so far from encouraging disorder or disloyalty, he had uniformly inculcated submission to the powers that be, not merely "for wrath, but for conscience sake." Most probably too, he would again "reason of righteousness, temperance, and judgment to come," and speak "concerning the faith in Christ," as he had done before Felix. At all events, we may be sure that he would not lose the opportunity of making known the Gospel of the grace of God even to that cruel despot, that unjust judge, who "neither feared God nor regarded man," and who then ruled the world. And though Nero resisted every appeal to induce him to embrace the Saviour, yet doubtless even he *trembled*, like Felix, at the apostle's denunciations of sin, and felt the excruciating pangs of a guilty conscience.

Why such a man as Nero should have pronounced sentence in the apostle's favour, it is not easy to explain. Probably, even his seared conscience was roused for the moment from its long and deep slumber, and compelled him for once at least to execute righteous judgment. No doubt also he had heard the favourable report of Paul which had been given by his own soldiers, and the "saints of Cæsar's household" who had become converts to the faith of Christ; for as Paul himself says, "the things which happened unto me have fallen out rather unto the furtherance of the Gospel; so that my bonds in Christ are manifest in all the palace." But whatever Nero's motive may have been, there is no doubt that Paul's appeal to Cæsar was now sustained, and that he was declared to be innocent of any charge, and was restored to liberty. Yes, the "Lord knoweth how to deliver the godly out of temptation." "If God be for us, who can be against us?" "He will keep the feet of His saints, and the wicked shall be silent in darkness; for by strength shall no man prevail." What a lesson to young men to fear God, and to banish every other fear. Let them adhere strictly to principle, and follow resolutely the path of duty, and commit their way to the Lord: and who is he that will harm you, if ye be followers of that which is good? "But if ye suffer for righteousness' sake, happy are ye."

II. Paul's Subsequent Labours.

Here the first thing to be noticed is, that the apostle, after his liberation, seems to have spent some time in Italy; and that, during this period, he wrote the Epistle to the Hebrews. At the close of that epistle, he says, "They of Italy salute you;" while he also mentions that his son Timothy, who had been apprehended and imprisoned, was now, like himself, "set at liberty." The epistle is addressed to those Hebrews who had been converted to the faith of Christ, but who were disposed to cling to the ceremonial institutions of Moses. It is very probable that it was addressed, in the first instance, to those converted Jews, who, when banished from Rome, had taken refuge at Corinth. The grounds of this opinion are very ably stated in an article which appeared recently in the *British and Foreign Evangelical Review*. But the epistle was evidently designed for all, in every place, who had been converted from Judaism to Christianity; and the main object of it was to prepare their minds for the approaching overthrow of the temple at

Jerusalem, and the consequent abrogation of the Levitical ceremonies, by showing them that all that had been typified by these was now fulfilled by Christ in His priestly sacrifice and intercession. Another object of this epistle was to warn the Hebrew converts against apostasy from the faith, and to support their minds, and secure their steadfastness, under the sufferings and persecutions to which they were exposed, at the hands of their unbelieving brethren. There seems to be no doubt that this epistle was written from Italy about the year 65, or five years before the destruction of Jerusalem by the Romans.

After leaving Italy, the apostle seems to have paid a hurried visit to Macedonia and Asia Minor, as he had intimated his intention to do, in the epistles he had just written to the Philippians, and to Philemon of Colosse. In these quarters, various errors had sprung up, which it required his personal presence and vigorous hand to expose and drive out of the Church. Then, he appears to have paid his long intended visit to Spain, where it is supposed that he spent at least a whole year, in preaching the Gospel, and organising Christian churches. Next, in the year 66, he appears to have returned to Asia Minor, in order to silence various heretics, such as " Hymenæus and Philetus," and Alexander, who had been sowing there the seeds of dangerous error. Then, he seems to have gone to Macedonia, and afterwards to the island of Crete; and returning to Ephesus, he at length finally left it, and proceeded, by way of Corinth, to spend the winter at Nicopolis; where, however, he was again apprehended, and sent a prisoner to Rome about the year 68. All this will appear more evident from the notices given in his epistles to Timothy and Titus; and it shows how active and unwearied Paul was in his Master's service to the very last; and how true it is that he "brought forth fruit even in old age."

1. The First Epistle to Timothy appears to have been written from Macedonia in the year 66, and probably about the end of that year. From the opening verses of that epistle, we learn that Paul had left Timothy behind him at Ephesus, in order to oppose and defeat the efforts of the false teachers, who had been labouring to subvert the faith and hope of the Church (i. 1-4). These Judaising teachers laid great stress upon the ceremonies of the Mosaic law, and denied the doctrine of justification by faith alone; and Timothy was furnished in this epistle with ample authority to denounce and condemn these ritualists, and prevent the contagion of their destructive heresy from spreading throughout the Church. It appears also that Paul, at this time, expected soon to see Timothy himself at Ephesus (iii. 14).

2. Shortly after this, the Epistle to Titus was written, probably from Nicopolis, a town of Ephesus, in the west of Macedonia, where Paul had determined to

spend the winter. After joining Timothy at Ephesus, it appears that Paul went south to the island of Crete, along with Titus, in order to oppose the false teachers there, and confirm the minds of the disciples. But as his time was limited, he left Titus at Crete, as his representative, to refute prevailing errors, to appoint qualified ministers, with the "laying on of the hands of the presbytery," and to promote the order and organisation of the churches. As great disorders had evidently prevailed, it required a firm and strong hand to repress them (i. 1-5). On leaving Crete, Paul seems to have proceeded to Corinth, and then, as we have said, to Nicopolis, where he intended to winter, and to employ his time in spreading "round about unto Illyricum" the glad tidings of salvation. His route at this time is indicated in Titus iii. 12, 13; and also in 2 Tim. iv. 20, 21.

3. Some time after the apostle reached his winter quarters at Nicopolis, his enemies lodged a complaint or charge against him, so that he was again apprehended and brought as a prisoner to Rome in the year 67 or 68. The word Nicopolis means the "City of Victory." It was built by Augustus Cæsar, in commemoration of the celebrated and decisive battle of Actium. There then it was that the apostle, after his numerous victories over heathen idolatry and Jewish unbelief, spent the last of his time on earth in freedom, and closed his public labours as a preacher of the everlast-

ing Gospel. At this trying time, there were few who had courage to stand by him. Demas, terrified at his arrest, forsook him now, "having loved this present world:" and none but Luke seems to have cast in his lot with the aged apostle, and accompanied him to Rome. Where then was Peter, whom the Papists regard as the first Bishop or Pope of Rome? Certainly he was not there at this time; and there is no sure ground for believing that he ever was there at all. If he had been there, it is not likely that Paul, in his last imprisonment, would have had cause to say, "Only Luke is with me." All the points now referred to are noticed in 2 Tim. iv. 9-15.

III. Paul's Second Trial and Martyrdom.

The Second Epistle to Timothy was evidently written from his prison at Rome, and shortly before his martyrdom. This second imprisonment was much more trying and severe than the first. Paul was not only chained to a soldier now, but he was closely confined in a dungeon, and subjected to many hardships and privations. Hence probably the reason why he asked Timothy to bring to him "the cloak which he left at Troas," to protect him from the cold of his damp and dreary cell. "I suffer trouble, as an evil-doer" (he pathetically says), "even unto bonds; but the Word of God is not bound" (ii. 9). The charges preferred against him seem to have been, not only that he sought to introduce a new religion, but that he had taken part in instigating the burning of Rome, a few years before; for which a great multitude of Christians, as Tacitus informs us, had already suffered death there; although, as that historian also relates, the guilty party was strongly suspected to be Nero himself. It is supposed that it was "Alexander the coppersmith" who had falsely accused the apostle of this crime (2 Tim. iv. 14). The apostle was now to be tried, not by the emperor, but by the city magistrates, from whom no mercy could be expected, on account of the popular hatred which was then turned against all who professed the Christian faith.

When Paul was arraigned before the Roman court, he had none to stand by him and plead his cause; but he had a powerful though invisible Advocate at his side, who, though He did not deliver him from death, strengthened him to meet death calmly and fearlessly. "At my first answer" (he says) "no man stood with me, but all men forsook me: I pray God that it may not be laid to their charge. Notwithstanding the Lord stood with me, and strengthened me; that by me the preaching might be fully known, and that all the Gentiles might hear: and I was delivered out of the mouth of the lion" (2 Tim. iv. 16, 17). From these words it appears that the charges made against the apostle at this time were not substantiated. He was not therefore condemned to death, but he was remanded to his dungeon to await a second examination and trial. Meanwhile, in the interval, he wrote to his beloved Timothy to "do his diligence to come to him shortly;" which, it is to be hoped, he was enabled to do, in order to comfort and cheer the aged apostle's heart in his last hours on earth.

The ancient Church universally believed that Paul suffered martyrdom at Rome in the reign of Nero; and as that emperor died in June of the year 68, the apostle's death probably took place a short time before that. His Roman citizenship exempted him from the fearful tortures which were usually inflicted upon the Christians, in that age of inhuman cruelty; and the apostle was condemned to be beheaded with the sword. He was led out to execution beyond the city walls, on the road to Ostia, the seaport of Rome, and near to the spot where the Protestant burying-ground now is. There, guarded by a body of soldiers, and passing through the crowded streets, Paul suffered, like his Lord, "without the gate." But death had no terrors for him; and he could now take up his own sublime song of triumph, "O death, where is thy sting? O grave, where is thy victory?" For mark his own emphatic words to Timothy, while he was yet shut up in his dark dungeon, and was daily expecting a sentence of death: "I am now ready to be offered, and the time of my departure is at hand. I have fought a good fight, I have finished my course, I have kept the faith: henceforth there is laid up for me a crown of righteousness, which the Lord, the righteous Judge, shall give me at that day; and not to me only, but unto all them also that love his appearing" (2 Tim. iv. 6-8).

Thus died the great apostle in perfect peace, and in the sure and certain hope of a glorious resurrection and an eternal reward. It matters little where, or when, or how, the Christian dies. Though he may die a martyr's death amid indignity and cruelty, and be buried in a felon's grave; yet, sustained by Divine grace, and by the prospect of future glory, he can encounter the king of terrors with holy tranquillity and exulting triumph. Though, like Elijah, he may be taken away as in a whirlwind and a chariot of fire, yet they will bring him safely to that better country where "the wicked cease from troubling, and the weary are at rest." "Blessed are the dead who die in the Lord from henceforth: Yea, saith the Spirit, that they may rest from their labours; and their works do follow them." In their case it is literally true that "the day of death is better than the day of one's birth." It is not so indeed to all, for to an ungodly man it is better to be born into this world, where salvation is within his reach, than to pass unsaved into the eternal world. But it is quite different in the case of the righteous; for the day of his *birth* was the beginning of many sore trials, and heavy sorrows, and anxious conflicts with sin and Satan. But the day of his *death* puts a final end to all sorrow and suffering, and introduces him to endless bliss. As to him to live was Christ, so to die is gain. When a child is born into the world, the parents and friends naturally rejoice; but if that child is born to a life of pain and sorrow, and if, when it dies, it passes into an eternity of woe, such a birth, if we could foresee all its subsequent misery, would produce not joy but grief unutterable. But the righteous hath hope in his death—the hope of a crown of glory; and therefore the day of *his* death is far better than the day of his birth.

It is not improbable that the apostle's body was buried in the celebrated *catacombs* of Rome, those vast subterranean labyrinths, where, through many ages of persecution, the suffering Church "found a refuge for the living, and a sepulchre for the dead." These catacombs are immense excavations beneath the city, and were first made about a hundred years before this time, in order to obtain a kind of earth or sand, which was employed in making the Roman cement. We are told that this sand was worked out in galleries, about two yards in height, and one yard in breadth, and many miles in length; while at intervals there were larger spaces, which were used as chambers for the workmen to rest in. To these galleries and chambers the primitive Christians fled for shelter from the persecutor's fury. Recently, entire skeletons have been discovered there, and there is no doubt that these are the mortal remains of Christians, because the heathens of Rome did not usually bury the bodies of the dead, but burned them in the fire, and preserved their ashes in urns. The Christians, however, buried their dead, because they cherished the hope of the resurrection of the body.

On these tombs, the inscriptions, which are still to be found, bear ample and striking testimony to the faith and hope of the early Roman Church. These inscriptions are very numerous, and are characterised by great simplicity and beauty. One of them runs in these terms: "Laurence to his son Severus, borne away by angels on the seventh Ides of January." Another, of the year 161, is as follows: "In Christ, Alexander is not dead, but lives beyond the stars, and his body rests in this tomb. . . . O sad times! in which sacred rites and prayers, even in caverns, afford no protection to us. When they could not be buried by friends and relations, at length they sparkle in heaven. He has scarcely lived who has lived in Christian times." It was, then, in these catacombs, that the early Christians found a refuge from the storm of persecution. There they might remain for months and years, as numerous wells and springs of water have been discovered in them. There also, in these "dens and caves of the earth," Christian worship was celebrated by prayers, and praises, and Scripture teaching. And it is worthy of notice that all the inscriptions on the tombs of these early believers and Christian martyrs, bear the fullest testimony to the scriptural simplicity and purity of the Church's faith in these primitive times. In none of them can any trace be found of papal supremacy, or of the worship of Mary, or of purgatory, or of prayers for the dead. There, in these solemn recesses, as has been eloquently said, we "meet with none but Christ; Him first, Him last, Him midst, Him without end. And thus, beneath Rome herself, there is the strongest testimony given against her corruptions of Christianity. The faith of the early martyrs was not the faith of the Papacy, but the faith of Paul, the faith of holy Scripture, the faith of Christ. Yes, Rome herself has, in the catacombs, evidence clear and unambiguous, of her departure from the early faith; and she bears within herself the memorial of a pure Christian worship, graven on the tombs of the first Christians with an iron pen, in the rock for ever."

Thither it was, in all probability, that the lifeless body of Paul was conveyed by his mourning fellow-disciples, to be laid in its last earthly resting-place; and thence he will come forth, on the resurrection morn, with his numerous spiritual offspring, to say in the presence of the Lord, "Behold me, and the children whom Thou hast given me." Then he will no longer be weary and worn, oppressed and persecuted, hated and reviled, and hunted like a beast of prey; but all tears will be wiped away, all sorrow will cease, all danger will vanish, and death itself shall die. Who would not wish to stand in Paul's lot at the end of the days? Who would not prefer, to all earthly pleasures and treasures, that crown of glory which adorns the apostle's brow? Young men, after Christ, take Paul as your model, and seek that promised grace which made him what he was, and which can make you like him, in all those moral excellences and virtues which ennobled his character, and made him a burning and shining light. But let no one hope to die the death of the righteous, unless he lives the life of the righteous, and becomes personally righteous by the justifying merits of Christ, and the sanctifying grace of His Holy Spirit. In the state in which death leaves us, in that same state eternity will find us; "for as the tree falleth, so must it lie." He that soweth to the flesh here, shall of the flesh reap corruption there; but he that soweth to the Spirit shall of the Spirit reap life everlasting. Let us then make sure of salvation by accepting Christ as our only Saviour, and trusting in His precious blood to wash our guilt away, and relying on His promised grace to make us what we ought to be, and what God would have us to be.

> "Hark! universal nature shook and groaned,
> 'Tis the last trumpet—see the Judge enthroned!

The Life of Faith.

Rouse all your courage at your utmost need,
Now summon every virtue, stand and plead.
What! Silent? Is your boasting heard no more?
That self-renouncing wisdom, learned before,
Had shed immortal glories on your brow,
Which all your virtues cannot purchase *now*.
 ' All joy to the believer! He can speak—
Trembling yet happy, confident yet meek:
' Since the dear hour (O Saviour) that brought me to Thy foot,
And cut up all my follies by the root,
I never trusted in an arm but *Thine*,
Nor hoped but in *Thy* righteousness divine;
My prayers and alms, imperfect and defiled,
Were but the feeble efforts of a child;
Howe'er performed, it was their brightest part,
That they proceeded from a grateful heart.
Cleansed in Thine own all-purifying blood,
Forgive their evil, and accept their good;
I cast them at Thy feet—my only plea
Is, what it was, dependence upon Thee;
While struggling in the vale of tears below,
That never failed, nor shall it fail me now.'
. . . . .

Angelic gratulations rend the skies,
Pride falls unpitied, never more to rise;
Humility is crowned, and faith receives the prize."
—Cowper.

CHAPTER VIII.

INNER SOURCE OF THE CHRISTIAN LIFE.

"To me to live is Christ."—PHIL. i. 21.

OUR remarks on the Life of Faith would be very incomplete without some reference to that inward root, that hidden source, from which it proceeds, viz., the life of God in the soul. We have endeavoured to present the leading features of Paul's character, in which seeming opposites are combined; such as humility with dignity, large-heartedness with tender-heartedness, unselfishness with conscientiousness, and courage with prayerfulness. And we have seen also how remarkably these high moral qualities were exhibited in the closing years of his life, and in the immediate prospect of a violent death. It is a rare spectacle, and a noble specimen of the power of living Christianity. What then was the *hidden root* from which these holy and abundant fruits were produced? What was that "well of living water" within him which continued to spring up so copiously unto everlasting life, and which poured forth rich, pure, refreshing, and fertilising streams on the moral wilderness around him? To these questions he himself furnishes the answer in the words, "*To me to live is Christ;*" and therefore he could add, "*to die is gain.*"

These words will appear the more remarkable if we consider attentively the circumstances in which he uttered them. It was during his first imprisonment at Rome: when, as we have seen, though he was bound with a chain, he had considerable freedom allowed to him, and had the privilege of meeting with his Christian friends, and even of preaching the Gospel to great numbers of people; and when his preaching was so successful in winning souls to Christ, "that his bonds in Christ were manifest in all the palace" of the Cæsars, while "many of his brethren in the Lord" were so stimulated by his zeal and success, that they "were much more bold to speak the Word without fear." That very success, however, had raised up against him many enemies in the Church itself; and more especially, it had brought upon him the enmity and opposition of the Judaising teachers, who insisted that the Gentile converts should submit to the burdensome yoke of the Levitical law. These men "preached Christ of envy and strife," in a spirit of sectarian exclusiveness and bitterness, and caused division in the Church by imposing terms of communion, which were inconsistent with the broad and expansive spirit of the Gospel. Thus, they sought to "add affliction to his bonds," and no doubt they added greatly to that burden of care, and anxiety, and grief, which pressed so heavily upon his mind. Then, too, the apostle was soon to be arraigned before the tribunal of Nero, to whom he had appealed against the unjust treatment of Festus at Cæsarea, and he could have little hope of mercy at the hands of an emperor, whose profligate life and bitter hatred of Christianity, and cruel persecution of the Christians, had made him the terror of his subjects. At all events, Paul, at this time, was quite uncertain whether his life was soon to be cut short by a bloody martyrdom, or whether he was still to be spared for further service in the cause of Christ and His Gospel.

It was in these circumstances, then, that he said, "To me to live is Christ, and to die is gain." His mind was alternating between fear and hope, as he looked forward to the future. *At one time*, he hoped that a favourable sentence would be pronounced upon him by the supreme court of the empire; and that it would still be possible for him to revisit the churches which he had planted, and especially his beloved brethren in the church of Philippi. Then again, *at another time*, the thought of a cruel and bloody death, to terminate all his earthly labours, would rise up before his mind, as more than probable. And yet, in this state of painful uncertainty and suspense, he was neither unduly depressed by fear, nor unduly elevated by hope; but he "possessed his soul in patience," and calmly acquiesced in the will of God, whatever that might be; and he was firmly assured that he would be borne triumphantly, through all his trials and conflicts, to a happy issue and a glorious reward. He was quite willing either to live or die, as the Lord might be pleased to appoint. "His confidence rested on a foundation firm as a rock, independent of the alternation of events, and unshaken by any waves or storms." No doubt, he had an earnest longing to depart from the trials and troubles of time to the pleasures and rewards of eternity, and to enjoy close and uninterrupted communion with his God, in the land of promised and perfect rest. But then, on the other hand, when he thought of his beloved converts, left as sheep without their earthly shepherd, he was quite willing for their sakes to continue longer in this world, in order to help forward their spiritual progress, and advance their meetness for heaven. Thus he was "*in a strait betwixt two,*" between his desire to "depart and be with Christ," which was far better for himself, and his desire to "abide in the flesh," as being more needful for the Church. But instead of deciding which of the two was best, he left the decision entirely to the all-wise Disposer of his lot, in the firm belief that whatever that decision might be, all that could happen to himself would redound to the glory of God, and promote the wider diffusion of the Gospel, and the highest welfare of the Church. In so far as he himself was concerned, he felt that it mattered not whether he was to live or to die; and he tells us what was the secret of his wonderful calmness, and of his profound submission to the Divine will, when he says, "To me to live is Christ, and to die is gain."

Let us then consider the real nature and the *inner source* of the apostle's life, and how this life enabled him to contemplate death, not only with calm tranquillity, but also with hope and joy. In other words, let us consider the secret source, or the hidden root, of living Christianity. "The kingdom of God cometh not with observation: for behold the kingdom of God is *within you*." It does not consist in outward forms or professions; but it has its seat in the heart: it rules in the inner man, and brings every thought and desire into captivity to the obedience of Christ. "The kingdom of God is not meat and drink; but righteousness, and peace, and joy in the Holy Ghost." It comes with power when the conscience is quickened to a true sense of the evil of sin, and pacified by the application of Christ's precious blood; when the heart is drawn out to Christ, in simple trust and sincere love; when the will is subjected to Christ's authority, and inclined to honour and serve Him; and when the whole inner man is brought into conformity to the mind of Christ, and consecrated to works of faith and labours of love. Such is living Christianity; and let young men especially consider attentively what is its true source, or its hidden root, and let them not stop short of realising a personal possession of it in themselves; taking Paul as their *Model*, and striving faithfully to copy it.

When the apostle says, "To me to live is Christ," he means to tell us that Christ was his LIFE, his true life. This true life he plainly distinguishes from his life in the flesh, or his mortal life here: for in the next verse he refers to his "*living in the flesh*," that is, his remaining on earth. Here, however, he speaks of a far higher life than this—a life which had its source or root in Christ himself, and which was manifested by his living and labouring *for* Christ, in the face of difficulties and dangers, and even death itself. He does not speak merely of life in general, or bare existence, but he speaks of that higher, purer, nobler life, which every Christian has in his soul, and which is truly the life of *Christ himself;* so that, as a living power in him, it moves and constrains him to think of Christ highly, to love Christ fervently, and to serve Him devotedly and unweariedly. *Life*, in the widest sense of the word, is of various kinds; and though it is a mysterious principle, yet wherever life of any kind exists, it always implies *activity*, or the power of producing certain results. For instance, vegetable life, in a plant or tree, is manifested by the unfolding buds, and the luxuriant blossoms of spring, and the rich and ripe fruits of summer. Then, animal life is manifested by the circulation of the blood, by the breathing of the lungs, and the other movements and activities of the body. Further, intellectual life is manifested by a wide and profound acquaintance with the mysteries of science, or the speculations of philosophy, or the letter of orthodoxy. Then, also, the natural life of fallen humanity is manifested by the love of the world, and the lusts of the flesh, and the practice of sin.

It is not, however, of any of these kinds of life that we are called at present to speak: but it is of *life in the soul*, or spiritual life, that "new life" which every true Christian has, and which he *manifests* more or less, by living not for time but for eternity, not to himself but to God; a life productive of all those fruits of righteousness, which are by Jesus Christ, to the praise and glory of God. *This* life, therefore, is an inner life, a "life hid with Christ in God;" but still, just as the living tree, which is full of sap within, sends forth branches, and yields fruits, which are patent to the senses, so the living Christian, who has the new life in his soul within, abounds in holy fruits—that is, in pure affections, and generous deeds. He is "like a tree planted by the rivers of water, that bringeth forth his fruit in his season: his leaf also shall not wither; and whatsoever he doeth shall prosper." Or, like a well of living water, this new life springs up in the soul, and sends forth copious streams of right feeling and right action, and so makes us holy in ourselves, and blessings to others. "He that believeth on me," said Christ, "out of his heart shall flow rivers of living water." What then is the nature, the source, and the aim of that new life, which is possessed by all who have a living faith in Christ, but by them alone? *To me* (said the apostle), not to every one, but to all who like me have found Christ, *to them to live is Christ.* What then does this mean?

1. First it means that the *Christian's life is from Christ.* That is to say, Christ is the source and giver of this new life. This was very plainly taught by our Lord himself, when He said to the unbelieving Jews, "I am that Bread of Life;" that is, I am that bread from which life comes to the dead soul; "for the Bread of God is He which cometh down from heaven, and giveth life unto the world." Common bread sustains the life of our bodies. Not only, however, does Christ *sustain* the life of the soul, but He *originates* that life in souls, which are naturally "dead in trespasses and sins." In short, He is the giver of all spiritual life, and the only Author of eternal salvation. And then He plainly tells us, that all the life which He gives to sinners, *comes from His atoning death;* for He said, "The bread that I will give is my flesh,

which I will give *for the life of the world.*" All this evidently means that, as Christ came to save the world, so the way in which He saves the world is by giving His life for our life, or by devoting Himself to death as a propitiatory sacrifice, and substitutionary victim, in the room of the guilty. "The wages of sin is death." That is the penalty which we have all incurred by transgressing the law of God. This penalty, however, has been inflicted, not as yet upon the sinner himself, but upon the sinner's substitute; and hence it is that "the gift of God is eternal life, through Jesus Christ our Lord."

Thus, our new life comes from Christ's atoning death; and it comes to us individually by a personal trust in His great sacrifice, and a vital union to Him who is pre-eminently "THE LIFE," as well as "the Way, and the Truth." Through this union, the believer dwells in Christ by faith; and he is so completely identified with Christ, that all his sins are imputed to the Saviour, and the Saviour's righteousness is imputed to him. For, as Christ identified Himself with His people, in paying their debts, bearing their punishment, and dying their death, so His people by faith, are identified with Christ; and thus they are treated by God, not as they deserve but as He deserved, and as if they had personally done and suffered what Christ did and suffered for them, "the Just for the unjust." What less than this can be meant by such utterances as these of the great apostle, "If we be dead with Christ, we believe that we shall also live with Him;" "I am crucified with Christ; nevertheless I live, yet not I, but *Christ liveth in me;* and the life which I now live in the flesh I live by the faith of the Son of God, who loved me, and gave Himself for me."

Such then is the *beginning* of that new life, which is the root and source of living Christianity. It begins in a personal union to Christ, and in the consequent enjoyment of complete pardon, and of true peace with God. And then the power, which unites the believer to Christ, is the quickening energy of His Spirit, which is put forth to rouse the torpid conscience, to subdue the proud will, to enlighten the dark mind, and to incline the perverse heart to receive and rest upon Christ alone for salvation. "You hath He quickened, who were dead in trespasses and sins." Once the believer was dead, under the curse of the broken law; but now he is alive in Christ, and therefore is freed from the curse, and reconciled to God; so that death has no more dominion over him, because his sins are fully atoned for, and all the penalties due to sin are for ever taken away by the shedding and sprinkling of Christ's atoning blood. Thus the Christian's life is *from Christ,* in its source.

2. But again, we remark that the Christian's life is *by Christ.* That is to say, his new life is sustained by the Saviour's grace continually imparted to him. To

all the living branches of the true vine, the Master says, "I in you." As the sap, which rises from the root of a tree, passes through the trunk into every branch, and thus sustains the life of all the branches, so Christ, by His indwelling Spirit, causes the streams of His grace to flow into the believer's soul, to sustain its life, and make it pure and fruitful. It is by no power in himself that this new life is maintained, amid the storms of trial, and the bitter blasts of temptation. "Not I, but Christ liveth in me." He is our daily bread, the bread of the soul, without which the new life would decay and die; but by which the believer gets power to do what otherwise would be impossible for him. The secret of his power over sin and Satan and the world is, that Christ lives in him. Once, he was led captive by Satan at his will, and it was a hard struggle to conquer sin, and it was distasteful to him to give himself to prayer and to holy exercises, and to deeds of piety and charity. But all this he now finds to be easy and pleasant; and why? Because Christ is *in him* by His Spirit, to strengthen him with all might, to fortify him against temptation, to change the whole current of his affections, and to enable him to abound in all good works. Therefore, conscious of his own inherent weakness, and contrasting what he once was with what he now is, he is forced to say, "It can't be I, but it must be Christ, who has wrought this blessed change in my soul, and who has given me such a dread of sin, such a tender conscience, such warm love to Him, and such an intense desire to do all the good I can, for the glory of God, and for the benefit of my fellow-creatures." All this he knows to be the very opposite of what he once felt and did; and the only explanation he can give of the change is, that his new life is sustained by Christ; and therefore, from what Christ has already done for him and in him, he is confident that "He who hath begun a good work in him, will perform it until the day of Jesus Christ."

3. Further, we remark that the Christian's life is *for Christ*. That is to say, his life is devoted to the service of Christ.

This living for Christ is the grand distinguishing feature in the character of all His true followers; and in none of them has it ever been more conspicuous than in the life of the apostle Paul. The great theme of his preaching was "Jesus Christ and Him crucified;" and his ruling aim was to bring sinners to the Saviour, and to persuade believers to walk after His holy example.* "We preach," he said, "not ourselves, but Christ Jesus the Lord."

His entire devotedness to the service of Christ is very manifest from what he says in Phil. i. 21-24. From these verses, to which we have already referred, we see that much as he longed for the peace and rest of heaven, yet he was quite willing to remain at his

Life for Christ. 143

post of duty and danger, for the sake of the Church. Now as to this, there are two very common errors, or two opposite extremes of error, into which even the true Christian is prone to fall.

The one extreme is, when he allows himself to become so engrossed and entangled with his worldly affairs, or even with his Christian duties, as to lose in a great measure that earnest longing for heaven, which he ought ever to cherish. "He so labours, as if his work on earth, which is but the commencement of higher energies destined for eternity, were to attain perfection here, or as if it were already the work of eternity." And so, forgetting that nothing here is perfect, and that this present life is a season of preparation for a better and higher life, he becomes so engrossed with the round of his daily duties, or it may be with his worldly concerns, that when death comes to call him home, it takes him by surprise, and finds him sadly unprepared.

But the other extreme, a very common one, is when the Christian's longing for heaven so possesses his soul as to make him grow weary in well-doing, slothful in his Master's service, and impatient to escape from the toils of conflict to the rewards of victory. He forgets, however, that when the Master comes, He expects to find His servants watching and working for Him, attending to every duty, and doing it thoroughly. Under the influence of this error many have retired from the world, abandoned their post of duty and honour, in the vain belief that they could better prepare for heaven in solitude and seclusion.

Now from both of these extremes of error the apostle Paul was entirely free. On the one hand, his untiring diligence, in serving Christ on earth, did not diminish his intense longing for the joys of heaven. And on the other hand, his intense longing for heaven did not impair his diligence in serving Christ on earth. Much as he desired to be with Christ, and to escape from all his earthly troubles and conflicts, yet he crucified this desire, and was willing to remain, for the sake of his brethren, and for the benefit of the Church. How truly then could he say that "to him to live was Christ." While he lived *from* Christ, and *by* Christ, he also lived *for* Christ, and he was ready to labour in His service till his latest breath, while at the same time he never lost sight of the glorious recompence of reward. Such then is the nature and the source of living Christianity. It is a new life derived from Christ, sustained by Christ, and devoted to Christ. And in so far as we possess this life, it will constrain us both to work and to *wait*—to work in the Lord's service, and to wait for the Lord's coming. "Blessed are those servants whom the Lord, when He cometh, shall find so doing." While our longing for heaven should not make us slothful in the Lord's work here, neither should our diligence in that work, nor any worldly enticement, diminish our longing to reach the better country, that is the heavenly.

From all that has been said, it is evident that, as the Christian's new life commences with the exercise of that faith which unites him to Christ, so this life is maintained by the continual exercise of the same faith; for "it is written, the just shall live by his faith;" that is, by his simple trust in the crucified and exalted Saviour. His faith is the living bond which unites him vitally, not merely to a dead Saviour, but to a living Saviour; and as, by this faith, he received righteousness from Christ at first to justify him, so by the same faith continually exercised he receives continual supplies of grace from Christ, day by day, to sanctify him, and prepare him for heaven. This faith alone can enable us truly to live to God, to live a life of holiness and a life of active usefulness. It alone can enable us to endure the trials of the world, or overcome its temptations, or meet undismayed the King of Terrors; for "this is the victory which overcometh the world, even our faith." A few years ago a man of great mental power was laid on his deathbed, and his friends, when they saw his end approaching, expressed to him the hope that his acute and powerful mind supported him in that solemn hour. "Oh no!" he said, "it is not my strong mind that supports me now; but it is simple faith, childlike trust in the Divine Saviour. But for this faith," he added,

"I would sink utterly in the deep waters through which I am passing, in the dark valley."

Yes, "the just shall live by his faith;" for he is "kept by the power of God *through faith* unto salvation." To many, and especially to the young, all this seems very mysterious, and even fanatical. But the "secret of the Lord is with them that fear Him, and He will show them His covenant." And yet it is not so mysterious after all, as many imagine. How then does faith enable the Christian to live to God, and to outlive all trials and dangers, and to conquer the last enemy? In answer to this, let me ask young men to weigh the following considerations:

1. Faith in Christ enables us to live to God, by *giving a new meaning to our life here.* What is the real meaning of that brief span of existence which God allots to us in this world? and how does He intend that we should spend it? Does He mean that we should act on the infidel maxim, "Let us eat and drink, for to-morrow we die?" Many, alas! seem to think so, from the manner in which their earthly life is spent, by "making provision for the flesh to fulfil the lusts thereof," by living only for themselves, by seeking their happiness in the polluted pleasures of sin, and shutting out from their minds all serious thoughts of God and of the coming eternity. They act as if they thought that man was made to eat and drink, to toil and sleep, to sing and dance, to weep

and die. And our great national poet has said, that "man was made to mourn," as if his life here were intended to be a burden, rather than a blessing to him.

But faith in Christ gives a new meaning to life. It shows us, from God's testimony in the Word of Truth, that man was not made to mourn, but that he was made to serve and glorify God, and to increase the sum of human happiness, by works of faith and labours of love. Man has made himself to mourn by forsaking God, and following after vanity and lies; and he can never truly *live*, as a rational and responsible being, until he has returned to God, and devoted his heart and life to His service. Faith in Christ shows us that true life consists in the conquest of sin, in the suppression of selfishness and of all evil passions, in the practice of virtue, in the imitation of Christ, in promoting the temporal and spiritual welfare of our fellow-creatures, and in extending the "kingdom of righteousness, and peace, and joy in the Holy Ghost." These are objects worth living for, and they are worth dying for, and it is only in so far as we make these the main objects of life, that we can be said truly to *live*. "She that liveth in pleasure is dead while she liveth." Those who idolise and pamper self, who seek only their personal gratification, who ignore their obligations to a redeeming God and Saviour, who seldom or never put their hand to any good work, and who make no earnest preparation for the eternal future, are utterly "*dead* in trespasses and sins;" and though they exist, yet they do not *live* in the true sense of the word. It is no better than the life of a vegetable or an animal, and it is just as useless for any good or holy purpose; nay, it is far worse than that; for their rational, accountable, and immortal nature stamps, upon their worthless and unprofitable life, high criminality in the sight of the unerring Judge, and exposes them to terrible retribution. But on the other hand, faith in Christ lifts a man out of self, out of sense, and out of the things of time; and gives him purer tastes, nobler aims, and loftier aspirations. It sets his affections on things above; it constrains him to use this present life as a preparation for a higher life, and to lay up treasures in heaven, which can neither be corrupted nor lost. "He that soweth to the flesh shall of the flesh reap corruption, but he that soweth to the Spirit shall of the Spirit reap life everlasting." Yes, according to the sowing here, will be the reaping hereafter. Faith in Christ, then, gives a new *meaning* to our life here.

2. But it also supplies a *new motive*. The motive is a sincere and fervent love to Christ. Every true believer can say, "Whom having not seen we love;" and "We love Him because He first loved us." Who can comprehend the "height" of that love to sinners which fills the heart of God's eternal Son, or the

"depth" of that love which led Him to stoop so low and suffer so much for our sakes and for our salvation, or the "length" of that love which extends from everlasting to everlasting, or the "breadth" of that love which embraces in its ample fold men of every colour and condition and character? But though we cannot fully comprehend Christ's love, yet the believer feels its constraining power in his own heart. Being forgiven much, he loves Christ much; and this love impels him to live for Christ, and to keep His holy commandments, in "the keeping of which there is a great reward."

> "Talk of morality! Thou bleeding Lamb,
> The best morality is love to Thee."

That love has a constraining power, an impulsive energy which nothing else has, or can have. Has it not enabled multitudes to fight resolutely against sin, and to meet death, in its most appalling forms, with patient tranquillity and triumphant hope? Has it not enabled them to subdue their own passions, to resist manifold temptations, and to "rule their own spirit," which is a far more difficult achievement than "the taking of a city?" Has it not enabled them to adhere steadfastly to the line of their duty, and to persevere in well-doing, amid obloquy and persecution, and even when there was no eye to witness their patience and constancy, but the eye of that Saviour, whom they loved so well? Listen to the testimony of one, who was once a daring blasphemer, but who became, through grace, a humble and devoted Christian:

> " The proudest heart that ever beat
> Has been subdued in me:
> The wildest will that ever rose,
> To scorn Thy cause, and aid Thy foes,
> Is quelled, my God, by Thee!

> " Thy will, and not my will, be done,
> My heart be ever Thine!
> Confessing Thee, the Mighty Word,
> I hail Thee, Christ, my God, my Lord,
> And make Thy Name my Sign."

3. Again, faith in Christ *imparts new strength* for enabling us to live to God. The difficulties of a truly Christian life are unquestionably very great, and it would be wrong, as well as foolish, to conceal or ignore them. It is no easy matter, in a world of temptation, to keep ourselves unspotted from the world, " to crucify the flesh with its affections and lusts," to cherish sincere love to our fellow-men, to do them good always, and to glorify God in our bodies and spirits, which are His. It must be the Christian's daily aim to reach perfection; and though he will never actually reach it till he dies (notwithstanding the vain imagination of certain modern dreamers, who fancy that they are already perfect), yet he must strive to be always coming nearer to perfection. It is a hard struggle; but it is not a hopeless struggle. For it is made easy to the just who " lives by his faith." By

faith he brings Divine power to his help; for by this key, he can unlock the treasury of heavenly grace, and appropriate its riches. By faith he realises the Saviour as very present, and near to all who call upon Him in truth; and it makes the Christian strong in His strength, and victorious by the power of His Spirit.*

What then is the chief lesson which young men should learn from all this? Should it not be their first concern to get that precious faith, which is the very life of the soul, and without which it is impossible either to please God or to live to God? Faith in Christ is the turning-point of a man's salvation, and the crisis of his spiritual history. It is the window by which the light of heavenly truth enters into the dark soul, and it is the living bond which binds the soul for ever to Him who is mighty to save. "He that believeth on the Son hath everlasting life: and he that believeth not the Son shall not see life; but the wrath of God abideth on him." Faith is the gift of God, and the fruit of the operation of the Holy Spirit, who not only convinces of sin, but who also enables the sinner to embrace the offered Saviour, as his own and his only Refuge. "Believe on the Lord

* For various suggestions in the four preceding pages, the author thankfully acknowledges his indebtedness to an admirable discourse, which he had the privilege of hearing some years ago from his esteemed friend, the Rev. Alexander Cusin of Lady Glenorchy's Free Church.

Jesus Christ, and thou shalt be saved." And continue to believe and trust in Him, and "according to your faith so shall it be done unto you, for all things are possible to him that believeth."

> " True Piety is cheerful as the day,
> Will weep, indeed, and heave a pitying groan
> For others' woes, but smiles upon his own.
> The free-born Christian has no chains,
> Or if a chain, the golden one of Love.
> No fear attends to quench his glowing fires;
> What fear he feels his gratitude inspires.
> Thought, word, and deed his liberty evince,
> His freedom is the freedom of a prince."
> —Cowper.

CHAPTER IX.

THE LIFE OF FAITH IN ITS PRACTICAL RESULTS.

"Therefore, my beloved brethren, be ye steadfast, unmovable, always abounding in the work of the Lord, forasmuch as ye know that your labour is not in vain in the Lord."—1 COR. xv. 58.

IN every part of the Bible, and more especially in the writings of Paul, doctrine is inseparably connected with practice, or life with action. In his various epistles, the vital doctrines of the Gospel are first of all clearly stated and powerfully enforced; and then the practical effects of the belief of these doctrines upon the temper of our minds and the tenor of our daily lives, are faithfully and minutely delineated. While inculcating the absolute necessity of a living faith in Christ, as the turning-point of our salvation, the apostle insists no less upon the necessity of proving our faith to be genuine by the practice of good works; and he shows that true faith "works by love" and "purifies the heart," and is productive of all the peaceable fruits of righteousness.

Thus, for example, after expounding the doctrine of the resurrection in his First Epistle to the Corinthians, chap. xv., he concludes with the following practical exhortation, verse 58, "Therefore, my beloved brethren, be ye steadfast, unmovable, always abounding in the work of the Lord, forasmuch as ye know that your labour is not in vain in the Lord."

To this exhortation and the motive presented for complying with it, we may now direct our attention in the concluding chapter, in order to see what the Life of Faith is in its practical results.

I. The exhortation: "Therefore, my beloved brethren, be ye steadfast, unmovable, always abounding in the work of the Lord."

The word *therefore* shows that this exhortation is not only connected with the preceding context, but that it is a logical conclusion drawn from the apostle's previous argument. The scope or design of that argument was, to show the reality of Christ's resurrection from the dead, and the consequent certainty of the resurrection of the just to eternal life. And, having conclusively demonstrated this, he virtually says, "Seeing that Christ not only died to atone for our sins, but also *rose again* from the dead to make us partakers of His own endless life, *therefore*, be ye *steadfast* in the *faith* of these great facts, and *immovable* in the *hope* which they inspire; and let this *steadfast* faith, and this *immovable* hope, stimulate you to abound always in the work of the Lord."

But to whom is the exhortation addressed? Not to all indiscriminately, but only to the people of God, or to those whom the apostle calls his " beloved brethren." For none but true Christians can feel the force of the arguments and motives, which are here urged, to a holy activity in the work of the Lord. Evidently, a man must *live* before he can be moved to action. There must be spiritual life in the soul, before that soul can be moved or drawn toward God, or impelled to energetic action in doing God's work and will. And yet mere life is not enough, but the life must be healthy and vigorous life. Even the true Christian, though quickened by the Holy Spirit, may become languid and listless in doing the Lord's work. And, therefore, he needs at one time, to be *warned*, by the terrors of the Lord, against besetting sins, and secret backsliding, and worldly conformity, lest after all he should be a castaway. And he needs, at another time, to be *encouraged* and stimulated, by the mercies of the Lord, to persevere in faith, and hope, and holiness, in order to reach the mark, and win the immortal prize. And this is what the apostle does in our text.

Now, the exhortation is obviously a very comprehensive one, and much more so than we might suppose at the first glance. It is comprehensive at once of the whole system of Christian doctrine, and the whole range of Christian experience, and the whole circle of Christian duty. It calls us to the sustained and vigorous exercise of these three cardinal graces, viz., Faith, Hope, and Holiness: *Faith* in Jesus Christ, as one who was not only dead, but who has also risen again; also, *Hope* of His coming glory, as it will be manifested on the resurrection morning; and further, personal *Holiness*, as the fruit and evidence of a true faith, and as the earnest and foretaste of future glory. Our faith is to be *steadfast*, and our hope is to be *immovable;* and if so, then our holiness will be exhibited by "abounding always in the work of the Lord."

1. "Be ye *steadfast*" in the faith of Christ. Now the word for *steadfast* signifies *settled* or *seated* firmly on a sure foundation. We say of a house that it is *steadfast*, when it is so compactly built on the solid rock, that neither external force, nor internal decay, can bring it down. And such ought the Christian's faith to be, not hesitating, or mixed with doubt; but firm, and strong, and steadfast. Many, however, deny that it is possible to attain such steadfastness in the faith as this, or that any one can feel perfectly sure of the great facts and doctrines of the Gospel; and they even make a merit of giving way to unbelieving doubts. But this is a strange and pernicious delusion; for why should we not feel as sure of the truth of God's Word, as we do

every day of the truth of a fellow-creature's word. People now-a-days speak of "honest doubts;" but in most cases, it would be more correct to call them sinful doubts. If we believe the testimony of man, surely the testimony of God is greater and infinitely more reliable. Men may err or deceive, and philosophical speculations may lead us astray, but God's Word is infallible, and can never mislead us; and if we take that Word, simply and submissively, as our guide, we not only may be, but we *shall* be, *steadfast in faith*. God's Word is a sure light to our feet, and a steady lamp to our path; and it is always shining, even in hours of deepest darkness, if only we would open our eyes to see its light. Wanderers as we are on a dark and stormy sea, and tossed often from wave to wave, we can never hope to reach the haven of rest, if we follow human opinions, or trust to the flickering light of human science; but we shall never be at any loss if we take God's Word as our guide, and give a whole faith to a whole testimony. That Word is infallibly sure and certain, a bright and steady light shining in a dark place. "He that followeth me," says Christ, "shall not walk in darkness," nor in doubt or uncertainty, but he "shall have the light of life."

Let us therefore be *steadfast* in the faith of Christ, and especially in the faith of His resurrection from the dead, and let us cherish a firm and unwavering confidence in Him who was once crucified, but who is now risen and exalted. Instead of being tossed by doubts as to the facts and doctrines of the Gospel, like a reed shaken with the wind, or like a wave of the sea driven about by every wind of false doctrine, or by every gust of sinful passion, let us seek to have a faith which is firm, and strong, and steadfast, like a house built upon a rock, so that no storm of trial will shake it, and no torrents of temptation will overthrow it. Realise the resurrection of Christ as a literal fact, and a most precious truth, and the very corner-stone of Christianity; and do not regard it as a doubtful speculation or a dream of the imagination. "If Christ be not risen, then we are yet in our sins:" for in that case, no atonement has been made for them, and there is no possibility of ever getting rid of them, but they must hang about us eternally, to sink us deeper and deeper in the abyss of woe. And is any one prepared for such a dread alternative? Better surely to get sin put away, and thus to be at peace with God by faith in Christ's atoning blood. Try to realise the bearing of this great fact, this vital and central truth—the resurrection of Christ—both upon your present peace of mind and upon your future prospects. Why should it not make our hearts glad, as it gladdened the hearts of the primitive Christians who, when they met each other in the street, were wont to salute each other with the words, "Christ is risen?" Why should we not seek to be as *steadfast* in the faith as they were? and why should we not regard His risen life as the pledge of our present reconciliation, and of our future blessedness? Does He not say to all who trust in Him, "Because I live, ye shall live also?" for "if the Spirit of Him that raised up Jesus from the dead dwell in you, He that raised up Christ from the dead shall also quicken your mortal bodies, by His Spirit that dwelleth in you." Be strong, therefore, in faith, giving glory to God. And the more "steadfast" you are in faith, the greater will be your peace, the brighter your hope, and the more abundant your joy in the Lord.

2. The second part of the exhortation is, be "immovable" in hope. This immovableness is opposed to wavering, or fluctuating between fear and hope, or vacillating between doubt and confidence. Now, hope is one of the fruits of faith, and it is inseparably connected with faith, and in some respects almost identical with it. The distinction seems to be this, that faith realises the unseen, while hope anticipates the future. Faith is the parent or source, for "faith is the evidence of things not seen, and the substance of things hoped for." The stronger, therefore, our faith is, the brighter also will our hope be; or, in other words, the more firmly we trust in Christ's promises, the more confidently shall we look for their fulfilment. And, besides, since *faith* has respect to Christ's resurrection, as the root of all vital religion,

so *hope* has respect to our own resurrection, as the fruit or result of Christ's rising from the dead. Therefore, if I have a *steadfast* faith in the risen and exalted Saviour, as one who is now at God's right hand, then I must also have an *immovable* hope that, being vitally united to Him, I shall yet rise and reign with Him in glory.

But how seldom is it that such a hope as this glows in the Christian's breast, to illuminate his path in this dark and dreary world! How often does his hope flicker and fail, like a candle burnt down to the very socket, instead of brightening the surrounding darkness with the rays of celestial glory! And why is it so? Why is it, that, while we are so powerfully influenced by worldly hopes, and stimulated to activity and energy by them, we are so little influenced by the powers of the world to come? The reason of it is, the *want* of faith, or, at least, the *weakness* of faith; for if we had a steadfast faith in Christ's death and resurrection, as the two great poles of a living Christianity, then we would also have an immovable hope of the glory which is soon to be revealed; and this hope in Christ would constrain us "to purify ourselves, even as Christ is pure."

It must be admitted indeed that it is no easy matter to maintain this hope immovably, amid the trials and temptations of this present evil world. There is much in our daily history, and in our earthly surroundings, much in our intercourse with the world, and in the corruptions of our own hearts, that is fitted to weaken and even destroy our hope of heaven. And, therefore, we should see to it, that our hope is really built on the only sure foundation, and sustained by constant supplies of grace from above. Let us not then be like the foolish man who built his house upon the sand, but like the wise man who built upon the rock. That Rock is Christ, and if we build upon Him, then our hope will be immovable, and His grace will strengthen our hope, and enable us "to read our title clear to mansions in the skies." And this hope will be an "anchor of the soul, both sure and steadfast, and which entereth into that within the vail; whither the forerunner is for us entered, even Jesus, made an High Priest for ever, after the order of Melchizedek."

3. The third part of the exhortation is, "Be ye always abounding in the work of the Lord." That is, be active and unwearied in serving the Lord, by doing His work thoroughly, and doing good to all continually; and whatsoever ye do, do it heartily as unto the Lord, and not unto men. Do all as under the eye of the Lord, so as to please and glorify Him.

Now, it is evident that this course of holy activity, in the work of the Lord, is the necessary result of a *steadfast* faith and an *immovable* hope: or, in other words, faith and hope are the mainsprings of holiness; for faith works by love, and hope stimulates to active exertion. The hope of wealth stimulates the merchant, and the hope of victory nerves the soldier with courage on the battle-field. And this faith and hope in exercise constitute what may be called the Christian's *inner life*, or the secret springs of a holy obedience; and then this holy obedience, in speech and conduct, constitutes his *outer life*, or the manifestation to those around him of his personal interest in Christ. As to this, we may quote a few words from one of Mr Moody's addresses. He said, "Christian people often ask me, What is the work I am called upon to do? Now the first work of all is to believe on Him whom God hath sent. First of all, we must be saved by faith in Christ, and then we must work not *for* salvation, but *from* salvation." And we may add that this is just what our Lord himself said to the Jews, when they asked Him, "What shall *we* do, that we might work the works of God?" in other words, how can we be brought into a right state of mind for serving Christ, and how can we get the requisite strength for doing the Lord's work? And what was our Lord's reply to the question? He said, "*This* is the work of God, that ye *believe* on Him whom He hath sent." This is our first duty, to believe in Christ; for "they that are in the flesh (carnal and unconverted) cannot please God." But by believing in Christ, as our atoning sacrifice, we get relief from that heavy burden of guilt which fetters our energies, and unfits us for serving God. And by the same faith also, exercised from day to day, we get continued supplies of grace, to maintain our energies in vigorous operation, and to enable us both to delight and to abound in the work of the Lord. And let it be observed that this is not a work only for ministers, but it is a work for every one who has found salvation. All are not obliged to become ministers, or missionaries, for all are not qualified for these offices. But every believer in Christ can find something to do for Christ, and he *will* find it, if only he is thoroughly in earnest, and is ready to do the work to which God calls him. God not only gives to every man some work to do, but He gives each man his own special and peculiar work.

But the apostle speaks of the "work of the Lord." And what is that? It is just the same *kind* of work as our Lord himself did on the earth. Not indeed His work of atonement; for in this He stood alone, and this no one can ever share with Him. In this respect, therefore, we *cannot* imitate the Lord; for His work of atonement is perfect, and it needs no supplement nor addition from us. But still we can, and we must, imitate the Lord in His *work* of holy obedience, in His service of loyalty to God and love to men. It was *His* very meat and drink to do His Father's will and to finish His work; and to this He gave Himself with unflagging zeal and untiring diligence. We can never forget how deep and tender was His compassion for the sick and sorrowful, and what kind and gentle words He spoke to the broken-hearted, and what generous deeds He did to all who applied to Him for help, and what meekness and patience He manifested toward His enemies, and how true it is that He "went about doing good." This then is "the work of the Lord" in which we ought to abound. That is to say, we must do the things which the Lord himself did, and we must do them in the spirit which animated Him. Well, then, we should ask ourselves whether we are really doing this work of the Lord from day to day? How is our precious time occupied? how stands our account with pleasure, or with business, or with God? What plans of usefulness are we forming or carrying out? what acts of kindness are we doing? what loving words are we speaking in our daily intercourse with others? Do we seize opportunities of doing good and of glorifying God? Let us ask ourselves such questions as these: and if we do so, it will show us how little we have yet done of the *work of the Lord Jesus*, and how much we have done to please ourselves, and promote our own honour, or profit, or selfish enjoyment; and this may well humble us, and constrain us to begin a new life, a life of faith upon the Son of God, and a life like that of Christ himself.

And then further, it is not enough to do the *work of the Lord* in a cold, careless, heartless way, but we must *abound* in it, or, as the word means, we must *surpass* or *excel* in it. We must strive to *surpass* ourselves, and to *excel* all our previous attainments, by aiming at the highest standard of Christian excellence, and the largest amount of service to the Lord. Nor must this work of the Lord be done only occasionally, or by fits and starts; but it must be done "*always*," that is, steadily and at all times, continually and habitually; "always abounding," and not merely now and then. In fact, this "work of the Lord" must be the grand business of life, always in our thoughts, constantly in our hearts, and never long out of our hands. Like the Lord Jesus himself, we must ever be "about our Father's business." As we can never go beyond what we owe to the Lord, so we must be striving always to do more, and yet more and more, for His glory; by abounding in deeds of mercy, and words of brotherly kindness, and gifts of Christian liberality; by sparing no pains, and grudging no sacrifices, to honour Christ and do good to all; and by putting forth every energy, and exercising every kind of holy influence, to advance the cause of truth and righteousness in the world.

But who, we may ask, is sufficient for these things? No one is sufficient in himself, but "through Christ strengthening us, we shall be able to do all things." Let us then not be scared by difficulties, nor even by dangers. If we look at all at difficulties, let us look with the determination to overcome them; and let us look more at our duties than at our difficulties, more at our obligations than at our hindrances and discouragements. A few years ago, a merchant ship was driven by a storm on the shores of Ireland, and stranded on the rocky beach. It was fast going to pieces, and the crew, seven in number, clung to the rigging of the sinking ship and shouted for help. The fury of the storm made it almost impossible even for the lifeboat to reach them, and none were disposed to risk their lives to rescue the sailors, till one man, more brave and generous than the rest, volunteered to go out alone to the foundering vessel. His friends sought to dissuade him, and said, "Don't you see the breakers dashing in foam and fury;" but he nobly replied, "I don't see the breakers, I see only the seven men on the rigging of the ship:" and so he went out and saved them all. It is in that spirit that *we* must do the work of the Lord. Let us not look at difficulties, but let us look at duties, and faithfully do them at all hazards, "always abounding thus in the work of the Lord."

II. The motive, or encouragement to *comply with the exhortation:* "Forasmuch as ye know that your labour is not in vain in the Lord."

"*Ye know this,*" says the apostle; but how did they know it? They knew it chiefly from the testimony of God, but partly also from their own experience as Christians. For it holds universally true that virtue is its own reward, and that those who labour for the

Lord, never *labour in vain*, and never have cause to rue their pains.

1. As to this, observe, first, that labour in the Lord is not *in vain*, because it *yields great present enjoyment*. It is not so with the labour that is expended on worldly pursuits, or lavished on sinful pleasures. When a mere man of the world has spent laborious days in realising a fortune, does his success make him a happy man! On the contrary, he is restless and dissatisfied, and still he craves for more. And though the votary of pleasure, or the victim of intemperance, may seem to be happy and jovial in the midst of his boon companions, yet conscience often troubles him, and makes him turn pale with its terrible warnings of coming woe. Listen to the testimony, which Solomon gave, as the result of his dear-bought and bitter experience, when he lived in folly: " All is vanity and vexation of spirit; yea, I hated all my labour which I had laboured under the sun. For what hath man of all his labour, and of the vexation of his heart, wherein he hath laboured under the sun?" What is it, in short, but labour lost, labour in vain, labour for that which satisfieth not? But it is not so with *labour in the Lord*, and for His glory. This is labour for that which is *above the sun*: it is labour for that which endureth unto everlasting life: it is labour of love, and work done for Christ. Such labour alone is worthy of an immortal being: it exercises his noblest

faculties, and develops his best energies: and in devoting ourselves to such labour, we shall find a great reward, in the testimony of an approving conscience, in the luxury of doing good, and in the gladness which springs from a sense of God's favour and blessing.

2. Then secondly, such labour is not in vain, because it makes not only ourselves happy, but it *makes others happy too.* When you sow the seed of Divine truth in the young, or speak to others about Christ and His salvation, and scatter friendly hints and kind counsel, you may be sure that the seed will spring up again, though it may be after many days. You may not live to see the fruit of your labour, but you may be sure that the fruit will appear either here or hereafter, on the shores, it may be, of another continent, but certainly on the shores of another world. At a meeting of the Social Science Association, the late Sir Richard Phillimore uttered these striking words, and not more striking than true. Speaking of the man who strives to diffuse the seed of truth, he said, "The seed which he sows may be long in the earth before it ripens, and he may never behold the fruit of his labour. The outward man perisheth, but the thought which he has uttered for the benefit of his fellow-creatures survives: the Lamp which he has kindled is not extinguished, but passed on to other hands, for the future welfare of mankind." Yes, "he

that goeth forth and weepeth, bearing precious seed, shall doubtless come again with rejoicing, bringing his sheaves with him."

3. Lastly, I observe that labour in the Lord is not in vain, because it *prepares us for heaven's eternal bliss.* Those who labour here in the service of sin, and who do the works of the devil, or who mind earthly things, shall eat the fruit of their own doings, and be filled with their own devices, in the gloomy abodes of misery and despair. But those who labour in the service of the Lord, and who abound in doing His work, are employed in what will constitute heaven's chief employment, and the chief source of its unspeakable felicity. By works of faith and labours of love for Christ, they are acquiring that character, and forming those habits, which will fit them for associating with holy angels and redeemed saints, who "serve God day and night in His temple." There is no idleness or sloth in heaven, but unceasing praise, and unwearied activity in doing God's commandments. In order then to prepare for heaven, "be ye therefore steadfast, unmovable, always abounding in the work of the Lord, forasmuch as ye know that your labour is not in vain in the Lord."

And now, brethren, " we commend you to God and to the Word of His grace, which is able to build you up and to give you an inheritance among all them who are sanctified." To the young we would say,

Remember your Creator, and give your hearts to the Saviour, in the days of your youth, and follow closely the Great and Good Shepherd, who gathers the lambs with His arm, and carries them in His bosom. To those of middle age we would say, Love not the world, neither the things of the world: lay up treasure in heaven, and choose the good part which will not be taken from you. And to those who are far advanced in life we would say, Go up through the wilderness leaning upon the Beloved; and when the eye grows dim, may the eye of faith grow brighter; when the natural force is abated, may you be strong in the Lord and in the power of His might. To those who are still strangers to the covenant of promise, and far from the kingdom, we would say, Seek ye first the kingdom of God, and make sure of a personal and saving interest in Christ. To those who are seeking the way to peace, we would say, Follow on to know the Lord, trust simply and exclusively in Christ's precious blood, and prevailing intercession, and powerful grace; and thus the heart of every one will rejoice that seeks the Lord. To God's children we would say, Grow in grace and in the knowledge of our Lord and Saviour Jesus Christ; cleave closely to Him, follow Him fully, and adorn His doctrine by a life and conversation becoming the Gospel. And, finally, to those who are parents, let us say, Cherish a deep and growing sense of your responsibility for the godly upbringing of your

Conclusion. 171

children; and strive by precept, by example, and by prayer, to train them in the nurture and admonition of the Lord,—so that, being grounded in the faith, constrained by the love of Christ, and animated by the hope of His glory, they may become blessings to yourselves, useful in their day and generation, ornaments of the Church on earth, and members of the Church of the first-born in heaven. Be ye therefore steadfast in faith, immovable in hope, and always abounding in the work of the Lord, forasmuch as ye know that your labour is not in vain in the Lord.

And "now the God of peace, that brought again from the dead our Lord Jesus, that Great Shepherd of the sheep, through the blood of the everlasting covenant, make you perfect in every good work to do His will, working in you that which is well-pleasing in His sight, through Jesus Christ, to whom be glory for ever and ever. Amen."

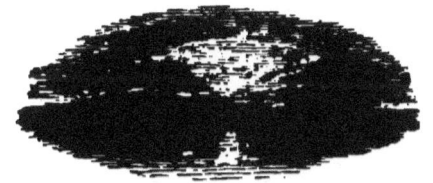

GROUNDS OF FAITH;

OR,

THE REALITY OF THE BIBLE MIRACLES.

"Yon cottager, who weaves at her own door,
Pillow and bobbins all her little store,
Receives no praise, but (though her lot be such
Toilsome and indigent) she renders much;
Just knows, and knows no more, her Bible true,
—A truth the brilliant Frenchman never knew;
And in that charter reads with sparkling eyes,
Her title to a mansion in the skies.
O happy peasant! O unhappy bard!
His the mere tinsel, hers the rich reward:
He praised perhaps for ages yet to come,
She never heard of half-a-mile from home;
He lost in errors his vain heart prefers,
She safe in the simplicity of hers."
—COWPER.

GROUNDS OF FAITH;

OR,

THE REALITY OF THE BIBLE MIRACLES.

INTRODUCTION.

THE QUESTION STATED.

IN this age of unsettled opinion, the question is often asked, especially by men of science, Is the Bible a revelation from God to man; and can sufficient evidence be adduced to show that it is?

Now these, it will readily be acknowledged, are questions of supreme importance, on which momentous issues depend; and they are obviously deserving of the most careful and serious consideration. And it is not less obvious that the Bible itself makes an authoritative claim, not merely to our reverent attention, but also to our implicit obedience. Moreover, the Bible professes to furnish ample evidence in proof of its Divine origin. Instead of demanding from any one a blind and unreasoning assent, it invites the most free inquiry, and courts the fullest investigation, into the nature and grounds of that evidence. Its language is, "Be ready always to give an answer, to every one that asketh you a *reason of* the hope that is in you."

Unquestionably, one of the most important evidences in support of the Divine authority of the Bible is the working of miracles, such as no man could have wrought unless God had been with him. This, indeed, has been questioned by some professed defenders of the faith, who have assigned an inferior place to miracles among the evidences of Christianity. It is true that this is not the only kind of proof that is placed within our reach; for there are others, both internal and external, such as the prediction of future events which no human sagacity could have foreseen, and the self-evidencing power of the Bible, which, like the sun, shines by its own light, and many more; and to these no small weight is due. But still, the evidence of miracles, if found to be valid, is obviously entitled to a high place in our regard, particularly as the Bible itself attaches special importance to it. "If I had not done among them," says Christ, "the works which none other man did, they had not had sin." When a king issues a proclamation to his rebellious subjects, declaring his royal will and pleasure, and offering to grant them an amnesty, he is naturally expected to take suitable means for satisfying them that the proclamation is not a forgery, but a genuine and authentic document. Accordingly, he subscribes it with his own signature, and affixes to it his official seal, to show that it has really come from him. The question then is, Have miracles, the broad seal of Heaven, been affixed to that proclamation of Divine love and grace, which the Bible professes to contain? If the alleged miracles were never performed at all, then it would follow that the Bible is "a cunningly devised fable." But if the miracles were really performed, then it necessarily follows that the Bible is true, and that it is entitled to be received by all as an express revelation from God.

This latter position it will be our object to establish to the satisfaction of candid minds. The field is obviously so extensive that we shall only attempt to give a bare outline, or what may be termed the mere *osteology*, of the subject. It may be remarked, however, at the outset, that there are three different words employed in Scripture to express what in our language is termed a miracle. These are *mighty works*, indicating supernatural powers; also *wonders*, causing astonishment in the spectators; and *signs*, proving Divine interposition.

CHAPTER I.

THE POSSIBILITY OF A MIRACLE.

IT is well known that some have affirmed that miracles are in their very nature impossible. And if this could be proved, there would be no need for any further discussion. But this daring assertion can easily be shown to be entirely without foundation. For it is obvious that our knowledge of God's existence and providence is derived primarily from the works which He has made. From the marks of design exhibited in the structure of the world, and in the adaptations of its various parts to each other, we naturally and properly infer that there is an Almighty Designer, a great First Cause. And not only so, but from the regular and uniform operations and processes of nature, we also infer that there are certain *laws* according to which the government of the world is conducted. And though our knowledge of the "laws of nature" is even yet comparatively limited and imperfect, yet we know enough to convince us that there is an established course in nature—a fixed order and regular succession in its various evolutions. But then, while all this is true, yet it does not follow that the uniformity of the course of nature must necessarily exclude the interposition of the Author of Nature, or prevent Him from altering that course if He should see good and wise reasons for doing so. "The laws of nature," as we call them, are nothing more than the *rule* or method, according to which God usually works; but these "laws" can never fetter or restrain His Almighty hand, or prevent Him from departing, when He sees fit, from His usual course of procedure. Nay, such departures from the "laws of Nature" as are implied in a miracle may have been predetermined by God in His eternal counsels, however strange or exceptional they may appear to our limited and clouded perceptions; and their very strangeness may have been designed to serve important moral purposes which could not have been accomplished in any other way. Even from the beginning, God may have so "ordered the constitution of the world, as to leave room for the exercise of those miraculous powers which He foresaw would at a certain time be exercised, just as He has left room for the free exercise, within narrower limits, of the human will" ("Aids to Faith," p. 21).

At all events, to assert that it is *impossible* for God to suspend or alter the laws of nature is manifestly unwarrantable and presumptuous. He who set the wheels of nature in motion at first, must surely have the power, at any time, to retard them or to stop them altogether. The denial of this would be equivalent to the denial of a Personal God, who governs the world which He has created; and it would lead to dreary atheism and pantheism. But, believing that there is a God, as nature through all her works proclaims, a God of infinite intelligence and glorious perfection, by whom the heavens and the earth were created, we cannot doubt that He can, if He please, alter or modify the laws which He himself has established. As Dr Paley truly says, "Once believe that there is a God, and miracles are not incredible," or impossible.

CHAPTER II.

THE PROBABILITY OF MIRACLES.

AS to this, it may be asked, Can any one affirm or prove that circumstances could never arise, under the government of God, to render it both expedient and desirable that He should give His fallen but responsible creatures an extraordinary revelation of His will? Is there anything incredible in the supposition, that, when a great and disastrous crisis in their history has occurred, God should make a direct communication to these creatures, in order to rectify their errors, and remove their sins, and guide them to peace and happiness? Man's urgent need of a Divine revelation has been conclusively proved by Dr Leland in his well-known work on the deplorable state of the ancient heathen world, when gross darkness covered the nations. So deeply sensible was Socrates, the illustrious Greek philosopher, of his own ignorance, that he expressed the earnest wish that a messenger could be sent from heaven to teach the world. And if such a messenger has really been sent down, is it wonderful that He should be endowed with miraculous powers to arrest men's attention, and to convince them that His message is Divine? And is it not expedient and desirable that " He who came as the conqueror of sin and death, and who had power to lay down His life, and power to take it again, should come also as the Lord of the Body and the Lord of the Spirit, having power over the elements of matter, and over the thoughts of men's minds?" An eminent modern philosopher has truly said that "the universe is governed, not only by physical, but by moral laws." " If, then, the spiritual restoration of mankind has in any degree been promoted by means of a religion professing to have been introduced by the aid of miracles, and whose whole truth is involved in the truth of that profession, we have a sufficient reason for the miraculous interposition, superior to any that can be urged for or against it, from considerations derived from the material world" (Mansel, p. 29).

CHAPTER III.

THE VALUE OF MIRACLES AS EVIDENCES.

GRANTING, then, that a revelation from God to man is both possible and desirable, the question presents itself, To *how many persons* ought such a revelation to be directly made? Should it be given to every individual in all the world and in every age? Or should it be given to a *few persons*, selected and commissioned to instruct the rest? Now, as to the first of these modes, it would, no doubt, be possible for God to reveal His will to every person separately. But we should feel greater difficulty in establishing the consistency of this mode, either with the wisdom of God, or with the free agency of man. Besides, such frequent revelations would soon lose their impression and their designed effect, and might come to be confounded with the ordinary light of reason and conscience. Obviously, therefore, the preferable mode would be to impart the revelation to a few persons, selected and accredited to be God's messengers to the rest of the world.

Here, however, another question arises, viz., How can the rest of the world be assured that these few are really commissioned by God, and that they are not giving forth merely their own fallible opinions? Now, while it would be presumptuous in us to assert that God might not have proved, in some other way than by miracles, the Divine commission of His servants; yet we may safely assert that there is no other conceivable way which would be more simple, more direct, and more convincing than the power of altering the course of nature by a word, such as that of dividing the sea, or bringing down bread from heaven, or raising the dead to life. None can deny, that "power" like this "belongeth unto God" alone, and therefore if He should accompany the message of His servants with such an exertion of almighty power, He would give the clearest possible testimony to the truth of their message, and "set to His seal" that it really comes from Himself. As no creature can arrest the working of His omnipotent arm, so every interruption in the established course of nature can only take place by His appointment, or by His permission. If the "laws of nature" were at first established by the great Creator, and if a human being is seen to accomplish such an alteration or suspension of those laws, as could neither be effected by human power nor foreseen by human intelligence, while that human being appeals to the miracle in proof of his Divine commission, is it not clear, beyond all controversy, that the miracle was wrought by the power of God, and that it bears most satisfying testimony to the truth of the message which he brings? Such, then, is the value of miracles as attestations of a Divine revelation.

CHAPTER IV.

TO WHAT EXTENT MIRACLES CAN PROVE DOCTRINES.

HAVING endeavoured to show, first, that miracles are possible; secondly, that they are expedient and desirable; and thirdly, what is their proper value as evidences of a Divine revelation, we come now to notice some of the leading objections of modern infidels to the reality of the Bible miracles.

But before doing so, there is another preliminary question on which it is necessary to make a few remarks, viz., How, and to what extent, miracles can prove doctrines to be divinely true? As to this, a difficulty has sometimes been felt, which, however, is more of a speculative than of a practical kind. The question has been asked, Can a miracle be wrought by evil spirits, or can it only proceed from the direct agency of God? And if it can be wrought by the former, how, in such a case, can the miracle prove the doctrine to be true? Now, though this question, viewed as one of pure speculation, or as a theme for metaphysical ingenuity, is attended with some difficulty, yet, as we shall endeavour to show, there is no serious *practical* difficulty involved in it. Instead, however, of dogmatising confidently on the theoretical question, let it be admitted, for the sake of argument, that it *is* possible for an evil spirit to work what may appear to be a miracle.

But if an apparent miracle may be wrought by an evil spirit, the question naturally arises, How can any miracle be a conclusive evidence of "the finger of God?" In answer to this, and in explanation of the difficulty, let it be observed that there are three conceivable cases in which a professed revelation may be given to man.

1. The first supposable case is that, in which a professed revelation bears, on the very face of it, obvious falsehoods, or contradictions, or immoralities; as in the instance of the Koran of Mahomet, or the lying wonders of paganism and Popery. Now, as to all these, it may be safely affirmed that not even an undoubted miracle, if it should ever be wrought, could prove such a revelation to have come from the God of truth and holiness; but it ought to be summarily rejected, as coming, not "from above," but *from beneath.*

2. The second supposable case is that, in which a professed revelation contains pure doctrines and correct morals. Now, in such a case, miracles would be sufficient to prove that God is its Author. If it give just and worthy conceptions of the Divine character, and if its morality be perfectly pure and faultless, then there can be no doubt that it could only proceed from the God of truth and righteousness.

3. But there is a *third* supposable case (and it is

actually, to a great extent, the case of our Bible), in which the subject-matter of the revelation is merely *above* our previous knowledge, by revealing new facts, or doctrines, of which we were not previously cognisant. Now, in such a case as this, miracles, we affirm, would be sufficient to prove the truth of the revelation, and to show that it really comes from God. For it cannot be believed that the all-perfect God would permit His power of working miracles to be employed by any being to deceive His creatures in a case where they have no means of judging as to the source whence the revelation proceeds. While no miracles could render it our duty to believe an obvious absurdity, or to practise a flagrant immorality, yet, in this third case, it would clearly be our duty to bow implicitly to the authority of the miracles alone, apart from all reasonings or imaginings of our own.

Nor, in arguing thus, can we be justly charged with "reasoning in a circle;" that is, with first making the doctrine prove the miracle, and then making the miracle prove the doctrine; as the advocates of the Papacy do, in arguing that the truth of the Bible rests on the authority of the Church, and that the authority of the Church is derived from the Bible. Such reasoning in a circle can prove nothing, except its own fallaciousness. But the case with regard to miracles, as proving the truth of doctrines, is totally different. What we affirm is, that if the doctrines of a professed

How Miracles can prove Doctrines. 187

revelation are self-contradictory, or its precepts immoral, then such a revelation cannot be proved by any miracles to be Divine. And further, we affirm that, in showing that the doctrines of the Bible are *not* self-contradictory, and that its precepts are *not* immoral, we do not necessarily prove them to be divinely true, but we merely render them *capable of being proved* to be so by suitable and sufficient evidence. We do not build a direct argument in favour of the Divine authority of the Bible upon the absence of contradictions or immoral teachings from its pages, but we merely clear the ground in order to lay the foundation for such an argument. And when we have got this length, when we have shown, as can easily be, and as has been shown to demonstration, that there is no real contradiction or immorality in the Bible, then the proof furnished by miracles is conclusive in favour of its Divine authority. Beyond all question, the Bible, in its every page, breathes a pure and lofty morality which, if universally practised, would change this sin-burdened world into a paradise of holiness and peace—a morality which, instead of thwarting or counteracting the force of the miracles, only superadds one miracle to another. And still more, the Bible, though composed in different ages, and by various writers, under the direction of One Spirit, is so self-consistent and harmonious in all its teachings, as to show incontrovertibly that these teachings have all come from one source, and that this source is Divine. Is it not, then, evidently true, that in so far as the case of the Bible is concerned, there is no *practical difficulty* whatever in applying the argument from miracles; but, on the contrary, as has been eloquently said, that "the miracles and the morality of the Bible stand side by side, and conspire together in showing that it comes from Him who unites the highest power with the highest holiness?"

CHAPTER V.

INFIDEL OBJECTIONS.

LET us now consider some of the leading objections of modern infidels to the reality of the Bible miracles. Here we are called to notice chiefly the well-known argument of David Hume, in his celebrated "Essay on Miracles"—an argument which has been employed by many other opponents of the Bible, and which has been substantially adopted by the late Professor Powell, in his essay "On the Study of the Evidences of Christianity;" although with this difference, that the Oxford professor went much beyond the avowed infidel in his opposition to miracles. The substance of Hume's argument is stated in the following words: "A miracle is a violation of the laws of nature; and as a firm and unalterable experience has established these laws, the proof against a miracle, from the very nature of the fact, is as entire as any argument from experience can possibly be imagined" (Essays, vol. ii., sect. 10). To the same effect Strauss says, "We summarily reject all miracles, prophecies, narratives of angels or demons, and the like, as simply impossible, and irreconcilable with the known and universal laws which govern the course of events." The argument of Hume seems to amount to this: Our experience of the uniformity of nature's laws has never deceived us, but the testimony of our fellow-creatures has often deceived us; and therefore he concludes that their testimony, except in certain cases, can never prove that there has been a "violation" of the laws of nature. He admits, indeed, with strange inconsistency, that human testimony might in some cases prove a miracle; but he maintains that if the miracle be intended to support religion, then no proof can establish its reality. That is to say, suppose that God should resolve to reveal His will directly to the human race, in order to remove their miseries and sins, and should think fit to convince them by miracles that He has really done so, then Hume would at once deny the reality of these miracles, and discredit the strongest testimony in their favour. Though the miracles might, in certain circumstances, be received as facts, yet they must be rejected as fictions, provided that they are designed to support a religion. In his estimation, a religious motive vitiates and evacuates the evidence furnished by miracles.

Such is Hume's argument; but if we closely examine it, it will not be difficult to show that it contains a double fallacy; first, in regard to *experience*, and second, in regard to *testimony*.

First, as to our *experience of the uniformity of nature's laws.* No doubt this experience may inform us as to past events, but it can give us no certain or infallible information as to future events. For instance, experience tells us that the sun has risen and set daily during the last six thousand years; but experience cannot make us perfectly sure that the sun will continue to rise and set for ever. Nay, if the observations of astronomers and the calculations of mathematicians are to be relied upon, it can be demonstrated that the solar system, as at present constituted, cannot last for ever, but that it contains within itself the elements of its own destruction. Again, suppose that the extinct animals which have been found imbedded in the rocks, and which belong to an era far anterior to the creation of man, had been capable of reasoning, they might have said, like Hume, "Our experience for many centuries shows that the laws of nature have never been violated;

and this, therefore, proves that these laws never will or can be violated." But the lifeless remains of these animals in the rocks show that their reasoning would have been as false as Hume's is, and that God did work a miracle to destroy *them* from the face of the earth. It is, therefore, nothing to the purpose to assert that a miracle is contrary to past experience. The only relevant question is, whether the evidence adduced in proof of the miracle, as a fact, be valid and sufficient or not? Neither is it true to affirm that "a miracle is a *violation* of the laws of nature," in any sense in which such a violation is regarded as impossible or inconceivable. For, as has been shown by Dr Brown, in his work on "Cause and Effect," a miracle is simply the introduction of a new cause, with new powers; and it cannot, therefore, be reduced to the rules suggested by a past experience, but its reality must be determined upon independent evidence of its own. For example, by the law of gravitation, all bodies left free fall necessarily to the earth; but by the will and power of man, aided by science, these bodies, such as a cannon ball, can be forced upwards in an opposite direction. This, however, is not a violation of a law of nature, but it is merely the introduction of a *new force.* If, then, man's will can produce such results, may not God's will produce greater? And why, in such a case, should our limited "experience" lead us to deny a fact?

This has been well illustrated, in a recent work, with reference to that mysterious principle of *life* "which seems to have the power, during its continuance, of 'violating' *all* the laws of nature. By that principle, the chemical elements which enter into the composition of the oak are detached from their natural connections, as they are found in the air, the earth, and the waters; the chemical laws which held them in these connections are suspended; they enter, under the new principle of *life*, into new combinations, constituting now the component parts of a tree—the organic structure, the fibre, the bark, the branch, the leaf, the fruit,—and they are held together, *by* that principle of life, with all the power needful to lift up the enormous mass from the earth, despite the law of gravitation, and to keep it steadfast against the influence of storms and tempests, century after century, until that principle of life shall lose its grasp, and become extinct; and then, not before, the chemical laws resume their power, and the old oak returns to gases and to earth, under the resumed operation of these laws. . . . All over the earth, therefore, on the land, in the waters, in the air, nothing is more common than that what are called the 'fixed and uniform laws of nature' are in fact suspended, 'violated,' held in check and abeyance, by this principle of life, where life is the only antecedent in the result. That a higher power than life—*the Life* itself, GOD—may not suspend them; that that higher Power may not suspend the laws which regulate life itself, or restore it, has *not* as yet been established by a firm and unalterable *experience*" (Barnes, "Evidences of Christianity," pp. 171, 172).

Second, as to *the reliableness of human testimony in favour of miracles.* Now, as to this, it must be admitted that *some* testimonies do deceive us; but then there is a kind of testimony which *never deceives us*, and the falsehood of which would imply as great a miracle as any recorded in the Bible. For example, as we shall endeavour to show in our next and concluding chapter, the testimony of the whole Jewish nation to the miracles of Moses, both at the time when they were wrought and in succeeding ages, cannot be reasonably accounted for, unless it was perfectly true. And so, the testimony of the apostles and others to the miracles of Christ, and the testimony of the primitive Church to the miracles of the first preachers of Christianity—miracles wrought publicly and repeatedly, appealed to as proofs of a Divine commission, and accredited by the losses and sufferings of those who performed and witnessed them—such testimony as this has a force and verisimilitude and conclusiveness which it is not easy to see how any fair reasoner can resist or gainsay. Those who bear testimony to these miracles could not be themselves deceived in plain matters of fact which they had seen with their eyes;

and neither could they have any conceivable motive to deceive others, as their proved integrity and personal sufferings amply demonstrate. Why, then, we ask, should such testimony, so truthlike and so consistent, be discredited or rejected, merely because the miracles which it attests were performed "in support of religion?" And yet Hume asserts that such testimony should be "rejected without further examination," merely because the miracles are the foundation of a system of religion, and because pretended miracles, or lying wonders, have been adduced in support of false religions, such as Popery. His argument just amounts to this: Some testimonies regarding religion deceive us; therefore all such testimonies deceive us, and none can be trustworthy. That is to say, because counterfeit money has sometimes been circulated, therefore we must reject all money as of the same stamp; whereas the counterfeit only proves the true. To assert that, because some testimonies are false, all must necessarily be so; or that, because some religions have been impostures, all must be the same, is equivalent to the monstrous assertion that because there is hypocrisy in the world, therefore there is no real virtue or integrity. Hume's argument is simply this: "Some men are liars, and *therefore*, all men are liars." King David said this *in his haste;* but he never said it, as the infidel does, in his calm and deliberate judgment.

We have already said that Professor Powell not only adopted the fallacious argument of Hume, but even went far beyond him, in his opposition to miracles. Hume candidly admitted that human testimony *might* prove a miracle, if "the testimony be of such a kind that its falsehood would be more miraculous than the fact which it endeavours to establish,"— unless indeed it were wrought "in support of religion!" And he admitted further that he would believe a miracle if he had seen it with his own eyes, and had been able to satisfy himself, by personal examination, that no deception was practised. Professor Powell, however, made no such admissions; but, on the contrary, he asserted that no kind of testimony whatever can prove a miracle: and he declared that he would not believe in one, although it were wrought before his very eyes. His own words were, "Testimony, after all, is but a second-hand assurance; it is but a blind guide; testimony can avail nothing against reason. The essential question of miracles stands quite apart from any consideration of testimony; *the question would remain the same, if we had the evidence of our own senses to an alleged miracle*" ("Essays and Reviews," p. 141). Such is the melancholy conclusion to which the so-called "reasoning" of modern infidelity is helplessly driven. This *reductio ad absurdum* is a suggestive commentary on the apostle's words, "Professing themselves to be wise, they became fools."

And the absurdity becomes all the more glaring in the light of this strange fact, viz., that while the doubting professor regarded all the miracles of the Bible as attributable either to mistake or deception, yet he professed considerable respect for the intelligence and moral character of those who, consciously or unconsciously, were guilty of these "pious frauds;" and that he professed also no small admiration of many of the truths which these miracle-workers taught and inculcated! Like Strauss and Renan, he thought that he could deny the reality of the Bible miracles without impeaching the honesty, either of those who pretended to work them, or of those who attested the reality of them with their blood.

Such, then, is the position which is taken up by the modern impugners of the Bible miracles. They endeavour to draw a distinction between the *facts* and the *teachings* of the Bible; and while they profess to respect the teachings or some of them, they utterly deny the facts, or miracles, on which these teachings depend for their truth and value as divinely inspired. But is it not clear to every candid mind that the facts and the teachings must stand or fall together? If a man professes to teach certain religious doctrines on Divine authority, and appeals to miracles in proof of his claim; and if I come to be convinced that he was "merely employing his superior knowledge of natural laws to produce a false appearance of supernatural

Integrity of the Witnesses. 197

power," I would at once reject his doctrines as an imposition. In attempting to explain away the miracles, and to ascribe them to natural causes or specious appearances, the infidel "deals a deathblow to the moral character of the teacher, no less than to the sensible evidence of his mission." For instance, if Christ professed to do many mighty works, and if His apostles professed to have seen Him and talked with Him after He rose from the dead, and if nothing of all this ever took place, but if it were a mere fiction or fancy, then how could we regard them as honest or veracious in teaching anything whatever? What confidence could we place in their truthfulness and integrity, seeing that they must have known whether the miracles were matters of fact or not? How could we believe in the moral honesty of men who attempt to palm doctrines upon the world by means, of what must be regarded as, on their part, a wilful deception? Such conduct could only be defended on the principle of the Jesuits, viz., that "the end sanctifies the means," or as Paul expresses it, " Let us do evil that good may come,"—adding the significant and terrible words, "Whose damnation is just." It is at least a consistent position on the part of the infidel to deny the doctrines of Christianity *because* he denies the miracles; but what must be thought of his position in denying the miracles and regarding them as deliberate frauds, while yet professing to believe, or at least to admire, the doctrines which these miracles prove to be divinely true? As an eloquent writer has truly said, "If the miracles are false or fabulous, the sayings of Jesus, which rest on them, lose all authority. It is vain to attempt a dubious explanation, which attributes to Jesus a half-designed, half-involuntary connivance in the superstitious ideas of His age. . . . This explanation shatters itself on the rock of an inevitable contradiction; for if Jesus was Himself deceived as to the line of demarcation between the natural and supernatural order of things, He was under no necessity to practise the convenient system of pious frauds. . . . Upon the second point—that veiled imputation of imposture, so much the more perfidious that it assumes the garb of eulogy—we can enter into no discussion. The spirit which confesses in Jesus, the Holy One of God, the great and solemn Witness of the Truth, repels with indignation the charge, and still more the apology. The moral sense is not different in the east and the west; under every sky it condemns falsehood, and cannot endure, without a shudder, the casting of such a blemish on the PUREST MORAL IMAGE THE WORLD HAS EVER SEEN" ("Jesus Christ: His Times, Life, and Work," by Dr De Pressensé, pp. 307, 308).

From all this, are we not warranted to conclude that the reality of the Bible miracles stands on an impregnable basis, which cannot be shaken or overthrown? We cannot deny the *possibility* of a miracle without denying God's omnipotence, nor its *probability* without denying His moral attributes of love and mercy. Neither can we deny the *value of miracles* as attestations of a Divine commission, without denying the instinctive convictions of every ingenuous and candid mind, that He who could raise the dead ought to be welcomed as a messenger from God. Nor can the truth and certainty of the Bible miracles be denied without destroying the very foundations of all human testimony.

CHAPTER VI.

ILLUSTRATION OF THE ARGUMENT.

THE most strenuous attempts have been made by modern infidels to disprove the reality of the miracles of Moses, in the hope that, if successful, they would shake our confidence in the truth of Christianity itself; seeing that the Old and New Testaments must stand or fall together. Each indeed has independent evidence of its own; but still, if one of these parts of Scripture could be proved to be false, the other could not hold such a strong position as it does. We propose, then, to show that the reality of the miracles of Moses rests upon an impregnable basis.

In considering the nature of those miracles which are ascribed to Moses, when he was in Egypt, at the Red Sea, and in the wilderness, it is impossible to deny that, if these miracles were really performed, they demonstrate the Divine origin of the Jewish economy. Any one can see at a glance that "these things were not done in a corner;" and also that they were of such a kind that no man could have done such things unless "God had been with him." There was no possibility of deception in the case; and if any had been attempted, it could easily have been detected. For the miracles were objects of universal, minute, and continuous attention on the part of the people, and they were patent to the senses, and exposed to the inspection of multitudes, during a long series of years. The deliverance of six hundred thousand men, besides women and children, from the bondage of Egypt, with a high hand and an outstretched arm; the dividing of the Red Sea at the lifting up of Moses' rod; the safe passage of the Israelites in the dry bed of the sea, with the walls of water on either hand; and the destruction of Pharaoh and his host by the returning waves:—then the thunderings and lightnings of Mount Sinai, at the giving of the Moral Law with an audible voice from heaven; the daily supply of manna in the desert during the space of forty years, and the gushing forth of streams of water from the smitten rock;—all these were miracles of such a kind as to exclude the possibility of mistake or deception, and to leave no doubt on the minds of spectators, that they could only have been wrought by the mighty power of God.

But then the question presents itself, Do the miracles of Moses afford *evidence as conclusive to us* as to those who saw them? Have we reasonable and sufficient grounds for believing that they are not fancies or fictions, but veritable facts? In answer to this, and in proof of the reality of the miracles of Moses, various reasons might be adduced; but of these we shall select the three following:

I. *The high moral character of Moses himself.*

As to this, numerous testimonies are borne both by Jewish and heathen writers; all of whom concur in declaring that Moses was a man of high moral worth, of transparent truthfulness and incorruptible integrity, as well as of great mental power and superior accomplishments. But besides these external testimonies, which are so well known that they need not be specified, his own writings clearly reveal his true character, and show that he was utterly incapable of fraud or deception. No one can read candidly the five books of Moses, without coming to the conclusion that he was a man who feared God, who entertained the most exalted conceptions of the Divine majesty and purity, who recognised God's omniscience, and revered His glorious holiness. And then, the great object of his life and labours evidently was to inspire all his brethren with the same lofty sentiments, and to persuade them to honour, love, and obey God, with all their heart, and soul, and strength, and mind. Still more, Moses was distinguished by the purest disinterestedness, by the most unaffected humility and meekness, by the warmest affection for his brethren, and the most devoted zeal for their welfare. With the great influence which he possessed and merited, he might easily have aggrandised his own house and family; but, on the contrary, he secured for them neither power, nor rank, nor worldly possessions, in that nation of which he was so long the acknowledged leader and lawgiver. Moses belonged to the tribe of Levi; but this tribe, instead of being exalted above the other tribes, had no share with them in the partition of Canaan, and was left in a great measure dependent upon their contributions. Besides, he assigned the high priesthood to the family of his brother Aaron, and thus prevented the possibility of his own children ever attaining it. And not only were his sons excluded from that spiritual office, but they were also denied the right of succession to him in his civil capacity; for he nominated Joshua, the son of Nun, of the tribe of Ephraim, to succeed him as the chief ruler and leader of Israel. In all this, then, we perceive a greatness of mind, a disinterestedness of feeling, and a purity of motive, which have rarely been equalled. Evidently he had no selfish ends in view, but his simple aim was to fulfil faithfully the high commission of Him whose servant he was. And who can read his dying testimony and parting charge to the people, without being convinced that such a man was incapable of deception or imposture? May we not confidently affirm that the infidel, who believes the contrary, manifests far greater *credulity* than that which he ascribes to those who believe that Moses was a man of God, and a messenger of heaven, and that he was proved to be so by "signs, and wonders, and mighty deeds?"

II. *The acknowledgment of the miracles by the Israelites at the time.*

The books of Moses abound with appeals addressed to the people, as to the reality of the miracles which they witnessed. These appeals not only prove the firm belief of Moses himself that they were real miracles, but they also imply a solemn attestation on the part of the people to the same effect. Frequently he had occasion to rebuke them sharply for their murmuring and idolatry and rebellion against God; but he never rebuked them for doubting or denying the miracles which they had seen. On the contrary, he employed these miracles of power and mercy as arguments and motives to induce them to love and obey God, who had shown them such distinguishing favour. Not only did the whole Jewish nation acknowledge the miracles as true, but it was expressly on that ground that they were persuaded to submit to the authority and guidance of Moses, to adopt the new institutions which he set up among them, and to conform to the burdensome religious rites which he enjoined. They were "a stiff-necked and rebellious people," as he often told them: they were most reluctant to abandon "the flesh-pots of Egypt," and were ever prone to break out into murmurs and complaints amid the privations and hardships of the wilderness; and many a time they would have been glad to find out that Moses was an impostor; and they would easily have found it out, if he had been so. But no suspicion ever crossed any of *their* minds that the miracles were a deception; and it was reserved for the rationalists of Germany, and their humble imitators in England and America, to discover and suggest this "*rational*" hypothesis! It cannot be denied that the contemporaries of Moses, that is, the whole Jewish nation, received the miracles as true and certain, that they handed down the record of them to their children as a reliable record, and still more, that they cherished the greatest respect

Acknowledgment of the Miracles. 205

for Moses during his life, and the profoundest veneration for his memory after his death.

Beyond all question, they regarded Moses as a chosen instrument, in the hand of God, to work out for them a great national deliverance; and on the ground of those miracles, which were performed before their eyes, they accepted the law which he prescribed to them, and submitted to that heavy yoke of ritualism which he laid upon them. And thus, in addition to the testimony given by the personal character of the lawgiver, we have the testimony of the whole nation to the reality of the miracles, which Moses performed by the mighty power of God.

It has been truly remarked, by a well-known author, that the history of God's dealings with Israel, especially at the Red Sea, was interwoven with the whole religious literature of the nation. "Living as they did apart from all maritime pursuits, yet their poetry, their devotion, abounds with expressions which can be traced back only to this *beginning of their national history*. They had been literally 'baptized unto Moses, in the cloud and in the sea.' . . . Even in the dry inland valleys of Palestine, danger and deliverance were always expressed by the visions of sea and storm. 'All Thy waves and billows are gone over me.' 'The springs of waters were seen, and the foundations of the round world were discovered, at Thy chiding, O Lord, at the blasting of the breath of

Thy displeasure.' 'They drew me out of many waters.' Their whole national existence was a thanksgiving, a votive tablet, for their deliverance in, and from, and through the Red Sea" ("History of the Jewish Church," by A. P. Stanley, D.D., pp. 123-128).

III. *The impossibility of persuading the Jewish nation, in any subsequent age, to receive the miracles as true, if they had been false.*

To illustrate the force of this part of the argument, let it be supposed that some learned pundit had recently composed and published a " History of Scotland," professing to give a true narrative of the doings and exploits of our Scottish forefathers during the last ten or fifteen hundred years. Suppose that he commenced his "history" by informing us that, at some remote period, our forefathers had come originally from France, numbering half a million of men, besides women and children, and a "mixed multitude" of strangers; and that they were under the direction of a great leader, who conducted them across the Straits of Dover on dry land, and who afterwards led them round, among the hills and dales of England, for forty years, by a pillar of cloud and fire; and that during all that time he gave them bread from heaven, and water from the rocks; and that he sent fiery serpents among them to punish their insubordination, and

Historical Aspect of the Question. 207

made the earth open her mouth and swallow up alive all those who disputed his authority. Suppose, further, that this historian, or romancer, informed us that, at the end of the forty years, our forefathers crossed the Tweed in a body on dry land, and then took possession of Scotland. And suppose, still more, that he also informed us that, ever since that time, the Scottish nation, at the request of the said leader, had offered up sacrifices, and kept solemn festivals every year to commemorate their ancient exploits, and observed a jubilee every fiftieth year, and a great many other ceremonies, which he described as being still the usages of Scotland. Well, would he be likely to succeed in persuading the nation that all this was true? Possibly there might be some credulous individuals who would believe it all; for in these days of Mormonism and spirit-rapping, there is nothing too absurd for some men to swallow. But would any man of common sense believe such a "history?" Would the whole nation believe it? Would they not say, "We never heard of such things before; our fathers never told us of them, and we find no such usages or customs prevailing amongst us?" And would not the almost universal verdict upon the learned pundit be, "Either he is a fool, or he takes us to be fools?"

This illustration may serve to show the utter impossibility of persuading the Jewish nation, at any period subsequent to the time of Moses, that the miracles were really performed by him, if they never were. To persuade them of this would require and imply at least as great a miracle as any of those which the infidel denies. For, passing from illustration to proof, let it be observed how the case actually stands. To indicate this, we may briefly advert to the *historical aspect of the question.*

Now every one knows that, at this moment, the Jewish people are dispersed among all the nations of the earth; not mixed with any, but separate from all, and still "a peculiar people." But go where you will, you find that every Jew not only glories in his ancestry, but reveres Moses, and receives his books as true, and regards them as "the oracles of God." This the nation has done, as all history testifies, during at least the last eighteen hundred years. During all that time they have generally, if not universally, read the law of Moses in their synagogues every Sabbath day; and the fathers have taught their children what they themselves had received from preceding generations. It may be said indeed that recently, infidelity has been making progress among the Jews, in some quarters. This, however, only proves the influence exerted upon them by their contact with those habits of thinking which happen to prevail in the particular land of their adoption. But it is something wholly strange and novel, as well as exceptional; and it can in no degree invalidate the harmonious testimony of the nation

Historical Aspect of the Question. 209

during the eighteen centuries which have elapsed, since they were in possession of a country which they could call their own.

We can, however, go much further back than the time of Christ, and trace the existence, and the recognition by the nation, of the five books of Moses, through all the preceding fourteen centuries up to the very time of Moses himself. For not only did Josephus write a history of the Jews, which embodies the leading facts recorded in the Old Testament, and the traditions which were current among the Jews previous to the destruction of Jerusalem; but about 280 years before Christ, the Old Testament itself (at the very least the Pentateuch), was translated from Hebrew into Greek by learned Jews in Egypt; and this Septuagint version made Jewish history familiar to the most civilised nations of antiquity, long before Christ was born.

Then, about five hundred years before Christ, being the period of the Babylonish captivity, we find that the books of Moses were not only in existence, but were well known and highly revered by the whole nation. For Zerubbabel, and Ezra, and Nehemiah, who at three different times led many of the people back to Jerusalem, rebuilt the temple, restored the worship of God, and regulated all the institutions of the nation, *expressly "according to the law of Moses;"* and they made pointed and solemn appeals to that law as their authority and rule, to which the people readily and heartily submitted.

Moreover, at a period still further back, or about seven hundred years before Christ, we find that the *Samaritans*, who occupied the places of the ten tribes after these had been carried away into Assyria, and who corrupted the worship of God by idolatry, revered the five books of Moses, and regarded them as Divine. And as there was bitter and constant enmity between the Jews and the Samaritans, the one would be a check upon the other, so as to prevent the reception of any spurious writings. Even at this day, on and around Mount Gerizim, there are those claiming to be descendants of the ancient Samaritans, who possess the Pentateuch, and who observe many of the customs and ceremonies enjoined by Moses.

Here also we may notice the remarkable confirmations of the truth of this part of the Bible history, which have been furnished by the explorations of Layard, Smith, and others at Nineveh, and more particularly by the recent discovery of the "Moabite Stone." This stone, or rather this triumphal tablet, the diction and spirit of which are thoroughly biblical, appears to have been erected by King Mesha to *Chemosh*, the national deity of the Moabites, in gratitude for the victories which he enabled them to obtain over the Israelites under Ahab (*circa* B.C. 896). The inscription on the stone, which is written in almost

Historical Aspect of the Question. 211

pure Hebrew, and which occupies thirty-four lines, both supplements and completes the record of the expedition by the three allied kings of Judah, Israel, and Edom, contained in 2d Kings, chap. iii.

Pursuing the same line along the course of history, we would refer to the contentions between the kingdoms of Israel and Judah, reaching back to the time of Rehoboam, or nearly one thousand years before Christ; and we would fix special attention upon the undoubted fact that both kingdoms, though frequently at war with each other, agreed in acknowledging the Divine authority of the books of Moses, as they had received them from their fathers; and, further, that in both kingdoms prophets were raised up, who in instructing the people and rebuking them for their idolatry, made their appeal to the *Law of Moses* as their authoritative rule and guide. Time would fail us if we were to notice in detail the numerous references by David, in the book of Psalms, to "the mighty works" which God had wrought by the hands of Moses, and which the sweet singer of Israel recounts as reasons for deep and abiding national gratitude.

This, then, brings us to three or four hundred years after the death of Moses. Now, at that period, what do we find? We find that Samuel the prophet, after Saul was anointed to be king, delivered an address to the assembled nation, in which he narrated God's gracious dealings with their fathers, in having "brought them out of the land of Egypt" by the hand of Moses and Aaron; and also "reasoned with them before the Lord of all the *righteous acts* of the Lord, which He did to them and to their fathers." Then further back, we find that, "when there was no king in Israel," but judges, whose authority was often limited to one or more of the tribes, it would have been impossible to get the whole nation, in its then divided state, to receive a false account of the events witnessed by their fathers; the more especially as all the books of the law were read in the audience of the people when they went to Shiloh to worship, and also as copies of the law were written out by the Levites and distributed among the people. And let it be specially observed that, during these four hundred years, the nation frequently forsook the law of Moses, and conformed to idolatry, for which God visited them with His judgments; but when they repented and returned, He sent judges to deliver them. But to what did they *return?* They returned to the *observance of the law of Moses.* But this they never would have done, unless they had been thoroughly convinced that Moses had been proved, by his miracles, to be a messenger from God; and unless it had been literally true, as the royal psalmist declares, that God "made known His ways unto Moses: His acts unto the children of Israel."

Such being the historical aspect of the case, may it

not be confidently affirmed that we have far stronger evidence to prove that Moses performed the miracles, and wrote the books ascribed to him, than we have for any past event recorded in ancient history? All antiquity, with one consent, and without one dissentient voice, bears testimony to the truth of his books and to the reality of his miracles. These books of the great lawgiver of Israel are quoted, or referred to, in various writings succeeding one another, from the earliest to the latest periods of Jewish history; and they are quoted, not merely as authentic, but as authoritative and inspired records of the laws and history of the nation. For instance, Joshua, the immediate successor of Moses, informs us in the book which he wrote, that he "read all the words of the law to the people. There was not a word of all that Moses commanded, which Joshua read not before all the congregation of Israel." And similar references will also be found in nearly all the other books of the Old Testament. Who can forget the solemn and affecting injunction which David gave, at the close of his life, to Solomon his son, "Keep the charge of the Lord thy God, to walk in His ways, to keep His statutes and His commandments, and His judgments and His testimonies, *as it is written in the law of Moses*, that thou mayest prosper in all that thou doest." But such quotations might be multiplied almost indefinitely; for, in truth, the entire Old Testament grew out of the book of the Law of Moses, as the branches grow out of the root or the seed. And to deny the existence of the law from the beginning, and to assign to it a later date, would make the whole history and literature of the chosen people an inexplicable riddle, a tangled mass of confusion; and would create greater difficulties than the infidel has ever adduced or imagined. On such a principle the truest history would be treated as a fable, and a field for indulging in the wildest conjectures of a disordered fancy.

But enough has been said to convince any candid mind, that on no other principle can the reverence of the Jewish nation for the books of Moses, during more than three thousand years, be rationally accounted for, except on the principle that *the events did really occur*, that the miracles were actually performed, and therefore that his mission was truly Divine. That mission bears upon it the manifest and unmistakable impress of Heaven's seal; and it is therefore entitled to that reverence and submission which are due to a revelation from God. These emphatic words of the ancient Jewish Church are most literally true: "We have heard with our ears, O God, our fathers have told us, what work Thou didst in their days, in the times of old. How Thou didst drive out the heathen with Thy hand, and plantedst *them;* how Thou didst afflict the people, and cast them out. For they got

Conclusion. 215

not the land in possession by their own sword, neither did their own arm save them: but *Thy* right hand, and *Thine* arm, and the light of *Thy* countenance, because *Thou* hadst a favour unto them."

We conclude with a single remark, and a short appeal. While, on the one hand, we cannot but estimate highly the value of miracles as attestations of a Divine revelation, yet, on the other hand, we would not unduly exaggerate their importance, or ascribe to them a power which they do not possess. Some who are wavering between faith and doubt, may be ready to imagine that, if they could only have seen a miracle with their own eyes, all their doubts as to the truth of the Bible would disappear. But even miracles, if frequently repeated, would soon lose their designed effect, and cease to make any impression. It was so with Israel in the wilderness; for though their whole history was a history of miracles, yet "they soon forgot His works," and "turned back," and "tempted God," and "limited the Holy One of Israel." No miracle ever yet changed a human heart; for though it affords clear evidence that God is speaking to us from heaven, yet it cannot compel us to *believe* the unpalatable truth which God declares to us. The great hindrance to the sinner's salvation is a moral hindrance; not the want of evidence without, but the *want of will within*, or what Scripture calls the "evil heart of unbelief." What we all need, therefore, is not more miracles, but more honesty of mind, more simplicity of heart, and more "power from on high," to bring us into a right moral state.

While, therefore, we give due attention to the credentials of Revelation, we must not neglect to study its contents patiently and prayerfully; and if we do search the Scriptures, we shall know that "unto the upright there ariseth light in the darkness;" for "if thine eye be single, thy whole body shall be full of light." And let us not forget, in dealing with such vital questions, the momentous interests which are involved in them. Surely it is the plain duty and the obvious interest of every intelligent and immortal being, to listen attentively and devoutly to Him, to whom Moses in the law, and the prophets, gave witness, and whose mighty and loving voice is still sounding through the ages, "I am the WAY, and the TRUTH, and the LIFE; and HIM THAT COMETH UNTO ME I WILL IN NO WISE CAST OUT."

LIST OF WORKS

PUBLISHED BY

JOHNSTONE, HUNTER, & COMPANY.

PHŒNIX BUILDINGS, 4 MELBOURNE PLACE,

EDINBURGH.

LIST OF WORKS

PUBLISHED BY

JOHNSTONE, HUNTER, & CO., EDINBURGH.

MAGAZINES—
    The Christian Treasury: A Family Miscellany.
    Edited by Dr Horatius Bonar. Super-royal 8vo.
        Weekly Numbers, Price One Penny.
        Monthly Parts, Price Sixpence.

    The Reformed Presbyterian Magazine.
    Published Monthly. Demy 8vo. Price Fourpence.

J. H. & CO.'S SABBATH SCHOOL TICKETS—
    Crown folio, printed in Colours.

    Sheet No. 1.—THE ATTRIBUTES OF GOD. 120 Tickets. Price Twopence.
    Sheet No. 2.—THE TITLES OF CHRIST. 120 Tickets. Price Twopence.
    Sheet No. 3.—THE PROVERBS OF SOLOMON—No. 1. 60 Tickets. Price Twopence.
    Sheet No. 4.—THE PROVERBS OF SOLOMON—No. 2. 60 Tickets. Price Twopence.
        Assorted Packets, Sixpence and One Shilling each.

J. H. & CO.'S PICTURE HYMN CARDS—
    Crown folio, printed in Colours, and Illustrated.

    Sheet No. 1, containing 20 Cards, 4½ by 3. Price Twopence.
        Do. 2, do. do. do. do.
        Do. 3, do. do. do. do.
        Do. 4, do. do. do. do.
    Packet No. 1, containing 50 Cards, 4½ by 3. Price Sixpence.
        Do. 2, do. do. do. do.
        Do. 3, do. do. do. do.
        Do. 4, do. do. do. do.

THE FOURPENNY SERIES—
Enamelled Wrapper.

THE SIXPENNY SERIES—
Extra cloth gilt.

Super-royal 32mo, Illustrated.

1. JEANIE HAY, THE CHEERFUL GIVER. And other Tales.
2. LILY RAMSAY; or, 'Handsome is who handsome does.' And other Tales.
3. ARCHIE DOUGLAS; or, 'Where there's a Will there's a Way.' And other Tales.
4. MINNIE AND LETTY. And other Tales.
5. NED FAIRLIE AND HIS RICH UNCLE. And other Tales.
6. MR GRANVILLE'S JOURNEY. And other Tales.
7. JAMIE WILSON'S ADVENTURES. And other Tales.
8. THE TWO FRIENDS. And other Tales.
9. THE TURNIP LANTERN. And other Tales.
10. JOHN BUTLER; or, The Blind Man's Dog. And other Tales.
11. CHRISTFRIED'S FIRST JOURNEY. And other Tales.
12. KATIE WATSON. And other Tales.
13. BIDDY, THE MAID OF ALL WORK.
14. MAGGIE MORRIS: A Tale of the Devonshire Moor.
15. THE SUFFERING SAVIOUR. By the late Rev. John Macdonald, Calcutta.
16. TIBBY, THE CHARWOMAN. By the Author of 'Biddy.'
17. OUR PETS.
18. THE TRUE CHRISTMAS. And other Tales.
19. THE BROKEN IMAGE. And other Tales.
20. FRED AND HIS FRIENDS.
21. THE STORY OF THE MICE; AND OF ROVER AND PUSS.
22. THE TREASURE DIGGER. From the German.
23. THE AYRSHIRE EMBROIDERER.
24. FRENCH BESSIE. By the Author of 'Biddy.'
25. THREE STRAY LEAVES.

THE DIAMOND SERIES—Price Ninepence—
Demy 32mo, cloth extra, Illustrated.

1. THE DIAMOND: A Story Book for Girls.
2. THE PEARL: A Story Book for Girls.
3. THE RUBY: A Story Book for Boys.
4. THE EMERALD: A Story Book for Boys.

J. H. & CO.'S ONE SHILLING SERIES (Enlarged)—
Small 8vo, extra cloth gilt, Illustrated.

1. THE STORY OF A RED VELVET BIBLE. By M. H., Author of 'Labourers in the Vineyard,' etc.
2. ALICE LOWTHER; or, Grandmamma's Story about her Little Red Bible. By J. W. C.
3. NOTHING TO DO; or, The Influence of a Life. By M. H.
4. ALFRED AND THE LITTLE DOVE. By the Rev. F. A. Krummacher, D.D. And THE YOUNG SAVOYARD. By Ernest Hold.
5. MARY M'NEILL; or, The Word Remembered. A Tale of Humble Life. By J. W. C.
6. HENRY MORGAN; or, The Sower and the Seed. By M. H.
7. WITLESS WILLIE, THE IDIOT BOY. By the Author of 'Mary Matheson,' etc.
8. MARY MANSFIELD; or, No Time to be a Christian. By M. H., Author of the 'Story of a Red Velvet Bible,' etc.
9. FRANK FIELDING; or, Debts and Difficulties. A Story for Boys. By Agnes Veitch.
10. TALES FOR THE CHILDREN'S HOUR. By M. M. C.
11. THE LITTLE CAPTAIN: A Tale of the Sea. By Mrs George Cupples.
12. GOTTFRIED OF THE IRON HAND: A Tale of German Chivalry. By the Author of 'Little Harry's Troubles.'
13. ARTHUR FORTESCUE; or, The Schoolboy Hero. By Robert Hope Moncrieff, Author of 'Horace Hazelwood.'
14. THE SANGREAL; or, The Hidden Treasure. By M. H.
15. COCKERILL THE CONJURER; or, The Brave Boy of Hameln. By the Author of 'Little Harry's Troubles.'
16. JOTTINGS FROM THE DIARY OF THE SUN. By M. H.
17. DOWN AMONG THE WATER WEEDS; or, The Marvels of Pond Life. By Mrs Charles Brent.
18. THE SUNBEAM'S STORY; or, Sketches of Beetle Life. By Mrs Charles Brent.
19. RICHARD BLAKE, AND HIS LITTLE GREEN BIBLE. A Sequel to the 'Story of a Red Velvet Bible.' By M. H.
20. LITTLE MISS MATTY: A Tale of the Sea. By Mrs George Cupples.
21. BESSIE BROWN, AND HER FIRST SERVICE. By Jane M. Kippen.
22. MARY'S WORK. By Hetty Bowman.
23. GENTLEMAN JACK. And other Tales.
24. THREE LITTLE GIRLS IN RED. And other Tales.

J. H. & CO.'S REWARD BOOKS—In Shilling Packets—
Enamelled Covers, and Illustrated.

1. PLEASANT WORDS FOR LITTLE FOLK. By various Authors.
   24 Halfpenny Books. Illustrated.
2. SHORT TALES TO EXPLAIN HOMELY PROVERBS. By M. H.
   12 Penny Books. Illustrated.
3. SHORT STORIES TO EXPLAIN BIBLE TEXTS. By M. H.
   12 Penny Books. Illustrated.
4. WISE SAYINGS: And Stories to Explain Them. By M. H.
   12 Penny Books. Illustrated.
5. LITTLE TALES FOR LITTLE PEOPLE. By various Authors.
   6 Twopenny Books. Illustrated.
6. CHOICE STORIES. 4 Threepenny Books. Illustrated.
7. JEANIE HAY; LILY RAMSAY; ARCHIE DOUGLAS.
   3 Fourpenny Books. Illustrated.
8. MINNIE AND LETTY; NED FAIRLIE; MR GRANVILLE'S JOURNEY.
   3 Fourpenny Books. Illustrated.
9. JAMIE WILSON; THE TWO FRIENDS; THE TURNIP LANTERN.
   3 Fourpenny Books. Illustrated.
10. JOHN BUTLER; CHRISTFRIED'S FIRST JOURNEY; KATIE WATSON.
    3 Fourpenny Books. Illustrated.
11. STORIES. By the Author of 'Biddy.'
    3 Fourpenny Books. Illustrated.
12. OUR PETS; THE TRUE CHRISTMAS; THE BROKEN IMAGE.
    3 Fourpenny Books. Illustrated.
13. AUNT LETTY'S STORIES. 3 Fourpenny Books. Illustrated.
14. STORIES OF HUMBLE LIFE. 3 Fourpenny Books. Illustrated.
15. HAPPY STORIES FOR BOYS. 24 Halfpenny Books.
16. HAPPY STORIES FOR GIRLS. 24 Halfpenny Books.
17. GEMS. 48 Farthing Books.
18. JEWELS. 48 Farthing Books.

J. H. & CO.'S 'CHRISTIAN CLASSICS:'—

Super-royal 32mo, cloth boards, - Per Vol., One Shilling.
Do. do. gilt edges, - „ Eighteenpence.

1. THE PILGRIM'S PROGRESS. By John Bunyan. Complete, with 8 Illustrations.
2. COME AND WELCOME TO JESUS CHRIST. By John Bunyan.
3. THE ALMOST CHRISTIAN DISCOVERED. By Matthew Mead.

J. H. & CO.'S EIGHTEENPENCE SERIES—
Super-royal 32mo, cloth extra, gilt edges, Illustrated.

1. SHORT TALES TO EXPLAIN HOMELY PROVERBS. By M. H.
2. SHORT STORIES TO EXPLAIN BIBLE TEXTS. By M. H.
3. THE STORY OF THE KIRK: A Sketch of Scottish Church History. By Robert Naismith.
4. LITTLE TALES FOR LITTLE PEOPLE.
5. WISE SAYINGS: And Stories to Explain Them. By M. H.
6. STORIES OF HUMBLE LIFE.
7. PLEASANT WORDS FOR LITTLE FOLK.
8. AUNT LETTY'S STORIES.
9. CHOICE STORIES FOR YOUNG READERS.
10. STORIES. By the Author of 'Biddy.'

J. H. & CO.'S TWO SHILLINGS SERIES—
Small 8vo, cloth extra, gilt edges, Illustrated.

1. ALFRED AND THE LITTLE DOVE. By the Rev. F. A. Krummacher, D.D. And WITLESS WILLIE, THE IDIOT BOY. By the Author of 'Mary Matheson,' etc.
2. THE STORY OF THE BIBLES. By M. H.
3. ARTHUR FORTESCUE; or, The Schoolboy Hero. By Robert Hope Moncrieff. And FRANK FIELDING; or, Debts and Difficulties. By Agnes Veitch.
4. MARY M'NEILL; or, The Word Remembered. By J. W. C. And other Tales.
5. ALICE LOWTHER; or, Grandmamma's Story about her Little Red Bible. By J. W. C. And other Tales.
6. NOTHING TO DO; or, The Influence of a Life. And MARY MANSFIELD; or, No Time to be a Christian. By M. H.
7. BILL MARLIN'S TALES OF THE SEA. By Mrs George Cupples.
8. GOTTFRIED OF THE IRON HAND. And other Tales. By the Author of 'Little Harry's Troubles.'
9. THE HIDDEN TREASURE. And other Tales. By M. H.
10. WATER WEEDS AND SUNBEAMS. By Mrs Charles Brent.
11. MARY'S WORK. By Hetty Bowman. And other Tales.

THE MELBOURNE SERIES—
Extra foolscap 8vo, printed on toned paper, Illustrated.

  Cloth extra, - - Per Vol., Eighteenpence.
  Do. gilt edges, - Do. Two Shillings.

1. THE COTTAGERS OF GLENCARRAN. By Letitia M'Clintock.
2. THE ROYAL CAPTIVE; or, The Youth of Daniel. From the French of the late Professor Gaussen.
3. THE KING'S DREAM; or, Daniel the Interpreter. From the French of Professor Gaussen.

THE MELBOURNE SERIES—*Continued.*

4. THE IRON KINGDOM; or, The Roman Empire. From the French of Professor Gaussen.
5. THE KINGDOM OF IRON AND CLAY. From the French of Professor Gaussen.
6. AUNT MARGERY'S MAXIMS: Work, Watch, Wait. By Sophia Tandy.
7. MARY BRUNTON AND HER ONE TALENT. By E. A. D. R.
8. LINDSAY LEE, AND HIS FRIENDS. By P. E. S., Author of 'Biddy,' etc.
9. QUIET TALKS WITH MY YOUNG FRIENDS. By M. H.
10. TALES FROM THE HOLLY TREE FARM. By Mrs Charles Brent.
11. TO ROSLIN: FROM THE FAR WEST. With Local Descriptions.

THE HALF-CROWN SERIES— | THE THREE SHILLINGS SERIES—
Cloth, plain edges. | Cloth, gilt edges.

Extra foolscap 8vo, with Illustrations.

1. ROSA LINDESAY, THE LIGHT OF KILMAIN. By M. H.
2. NEWLYN HOUSE, THE HOME OF THE DAVENPORTS. By A. E. W.
3. ALICE THORNE; or, A Sister's Work.
4. LABOURERS IN THE VINEYARD. By M. H.
5. THE CHILDREN OF THE GREAT KING. By M. H.
6. LITTLE HARRY'S TROUBLES. By the Author of 'Gottfried.'
7. SUNDAY SCHOOL PHOTOGRAPHS. By Rev. Alfred Taylor, Bristol, Pennsylvania.
8. WAYMARKS FOR THE GUIDING OF LITTLE FEET. By the Rev. J. A. Wallace.
9. THE DOMESTIC CIRCLE. By the Rev. John Thomson.
10. SELECT CHRISTIAN BIOGRAPHIES. By the Rev. James Gardner, A.M., M.D.
11. JAMES NISBET: A Study for Young Men. By the Rev. J. A. Wallace.
12. NOBLE RIVERS, AND STORIES CONCERNING THEM. By Anna J. Buckland.
13. THE HARLEYS OF CHELSEA PLACE. By Sophia Tandy.
14. VIOLET AND DAISY; or, The Picture with Two Sides. By M. H.
15. THE MELVILL FAMILY, AND THEIR BIBLE READINGS. By Mrs Ellis.
16. THE COTTAGERS OF GLENBURNIE. By Elizabeth Hamilton.

THE 'CHILDREN'S HOUR' SERIES—
Cloth Elegant, cut edges, - Per Vol., Half-a-Crown.
Do. gilt side and edges, ,, Three Shillings.

Complete in Twelve Volumes.

An admirable Series for the Family or for School Libraries.

1. MISS MATTY; or, Our Youngest Passenger. By Mrs George Cupples. And other Tales. Illustrated.
2. HORACE HAZELWOOD; or, Little Things. By Robert Hope Moncrieff. And other Tales. Illustrated.

THE CHILDREN'S HOUR SERIES—*Continued.*

3. FOUND AFLOAT. By Mrs George Cupples. And other Tales. Illustrated.
4. THE WHITE ROE OF GLENMERE. By Mrs Bickerstaffe. And other Tales. Illustrated.
5. JESSIE OGLETHORPE: The Story of a Daughter's Devotion. By W. H. Davenport Adams. And other Tales. Illustrated.
6. PAUL AND MARIE, THE ORPHANS OF AUVERGNE. And other Tales. Illustrated.
7. ARCHIE MASON: An Irish Story. By Letitia M'Clintock. And other Tales. Illustrated.
8. THE WOODFORDS: An Emigrant Story. By Mrs George Cupples. And other Tales. Illustrated.
9. OLD ANDY'S MONEY: An Irish Story. By Letitia M'Clintock. And other Tales. Illustrated.
10. MARIUS FLAMINIUS: A Story of the Days of Hadrian. By Anna J. Buckland. And other Tales. Illustrated.
11. THE INUNDATION OF THE RHINE. From the German. And other Tales. Illustrated.
12. THE LITTLE ORPHANS. From the German. And other Tales. Illustrated.

THE THREE SHILLINGS AND SIXPENCE SERIES—
Cloth, plain edges.

THE FOUR SHILLINGS AND SIXPENCE SERIES.
Cloth, gilt edges.

Crown 8vo, cloth, with Illustrations.

1. SKETCHES OF SCRIPTURE CHARACTERS. By the Rev. Andrew Thomson, D.D.
2. STARS OF EARTH; or, Wild Flowers of the Months. By Leigh Page.
3. ELIJAH, THE DESERT PROPHET. By the Rev. H. T. Howat.
4. CHAPTERS IN THE LIFE OF ELSIE ELLIS. By Hetty Bowman.
5. NANNETTE'S DIARY: A Story of Puritan Times. By Anna J. Buckland.
6. ETHEL LINTON; or, The Feversham Temper. By A. E. W.
7. SUZANNE DE L'ORME: A Tale of France in Huguenot Times. By H. G.
8. LILY HOPE AND HER FRIENDS. By Hetty Bowman.

J. H. & CO.'S FIVE SHILLINGS SERIES—
Extra foolscap 8vo, cloth, gilt side and edges.

1. THE CHILDREN'S HOUR ANNUAL. First Series. 656 pp. 60 Illustrations.
2. Do. Do. Second Series. 640 pp. 70 Illustrations.
3. Do. Do. Third Series. 640 pp. 70 Illustrations.
4. Do. Do. Fourth Series. 640 pp. 60 Illustrations.
5. Do. Do. Fifth Series. 640 pp. 60 Illustrations.
6. Do. Do. Sixth Series. 640 pp. 60 Illustrations.
7. THE STORY OF DANIEL. From the French of Professor Gaussen. By Mr and Mrs Campbell Overend. Toned paper, 450 pp. 5 Illustrations.

MISCELLANEOUS WORKS.

Authorised Standards of Free Church of Scotland: Being the
Westminster Confession of Faith, and other Documents. *Published by authority of the General Assembly.* Demy 12mo, cloth limp, - £0 1 6
———— Cloth boards, - - - - - 0 1 8
———— Superior Edition, printed on superfine paper, extra cloth, bevelled boards, antique, - - - - - - 0 3 6
———— Full calf, lettered, antique, - - - - 0 5 0

Brodie (Rev. James, A.M.) The Antiquity and Nature of Man:
A Reply to Sir Charles Lyell's Recent Work. Extra foolscap 8vo, cloth, - - - - - - - - 0 2 6

———— **The Rational Creation: An Inquiry into the Nature and** Classification of Rational Creatures, and the Government which God exercises over them. Crown 8vo, cloth, - - - - 0 5 0

———— **Our Present Position on the Chart of Time, as Revealed in** the Word of God. Enlarged Edition. Extra foolscap 8vo, - - 0 1 0
———— Cloth, - - - - - - 0 1 6

———— **The True Text of the Old Testament, with some Remarks** on the Language of the Jews. Crown 8vo, cloth, - - 0 3 0

Burns (Rev. Geo., D.D.) Prayers for the use of Sabbath Schools.
18mo, sewed, - - - - - - - 0 0 4

Calvin's Treatise on Relics. With an Introductory Dissertation
on Image Worship and other Superstitions in the Roman Catholic and Russo-Greek Churches. By the late Count Valerian Krasinski. Extra foolscap 8vo, cloth, - - - - - 0 2 6

Catechisms—
CATECHISM OF THE EVIDENCES OF REVEALED RELIGION, with a few Preliminary Questions on Natural Religion. By William Ferrie, D.D., Kilconquhar. 18mo, stitched, - - - 0 0 4
CATECHISM ON BAPTISM: in which are considered its Nature, its Subjects, and the Obligations resulting from it. By the late Henry Grey, D.D., Edinburgh. 18mo, stitched, - - - 0 0 6
THE ASSEMBLY'S LARGER CATECHISM; with (*Italicised*) Proofs from Scripture at full length. Demy 12mo, sewed, - - 0 0 8

Catechisms—*Continued.*

THE ASSEMBLY'S SHORTER CATECHISM; with (*Italicised*) Proofs from Scripture at full length; also with Additional Scripture References, selected from Boston, Fisher, M. Henry, Paterson, Vincent, and others. Demy 18mo, stitched, - - - £0 0 1

THE ASSEMBLY'S SHORTER CATECHISM; with References to the Scripture Proofs. Demy 18mo, stitched, - - - 0 0 0½

THE CHILD'S FIRST CATECHISM. 48mo, stitched, - - 0 0 0¼

SHORT CATECHISM FOR YOUNG CHILDREN. By the Rev. John Brown, Haddington. 32mo, stitched, - - - 0 0 0½

PLAIN CATECHISM FOR CHILDREN. By the Rev. Matthew Henry. 18mo, stitched, - - - - - 0 0 1

FIFTY QUESTIONS CONCERNING THE LEADING DOCTRINES AND DUTIES OF THE GOSPEL; with Scripture Answers and Parallel Texts. For the use of Sabbath Schools. 18mo, stitched, - - 0 0 1

FORM OF EXAMINATION BEFORE THE COMMUNION. Approved by the General Assembly of the Kirk of Scotland (1592), and appointed to be read in Families and Schools; with Proofs from Scripture (commonly known as 'Craig's Catechism'). With a Recommendatory Note by the Rev. Dr Candlish, Rev. Alex. Moody Stuart, and Rev. Dr Horatius Bonar. 18mo, stitched, - - 0 0 1

THE MOTHER'S CATECHISM; being a Preparatory Help for the Young and Ignorant, to their easier understanding The Assembly's Shorter Catechism. By the Rev. John Willison, Dundee. 32mo, stitched, - - - - - - 0 0 0½

WATTS' (DR ISAAC) JUVENILE HISTORICAL CATECHISMS OF THE OLD AND NEW TESTAMENTS; with Numerous Scripture References, and a Selection of Hymns. Demy 18mo, stitched, - - 0 0 1

A SCRIPTURE CATECHISM, Historical and Doctrinal, for the use of Schools and Families. By John Whitecross, Author of 'Anecdotes on the Shorter Catechism,' etc. 18mo, stitched, - 0 0 1

A SUMMARY OF CHRISTIAN DOCTRINES AND DUTIES; being the Westminster Assembly's Shorter Catechism, without the Questions, with Marginal References. Foolscap 8vo, stitched, - 0 0 1

Christian Treasury (The) Volumes 1845 to 1860.

16 Volumes. Royal 8vo. A complete Set will be forwarded to any part of the country, carriage paid, on receipt of - - 2 2 0

―――― Volumes 1861 to 1873.
Super-royal, cloth, green and gold—each - - 0 6 6

Cloud of Witnesses (A) for the Royal Prerogatives of Jesus Christ:

Being the Last Speeches and Testimonies of those who have Suffered for the Truth in Scotland since the year 1680. A New Edition, with Explanatory and Historical Notes, by the Rev. J. H. Thomson. Printed on Toned Paper, with Full-Page Illustrations. Demy 8vo, cloth extra, - - - - - - - 0 7 6

―――――― Calf, antique, red edges, - - - 0 15 0

Cochrane (Rev. Thomas). Home Mission Work: Its Duties,
Difficulties, and Encouragements. Super-royal 32mo, - - £0 1 0

Confession of Faith (The), agreed upon at the Assembly of
Divines at Westminster. Complete Edition, with the *Italics* of the Elegant Quarto Edition of 1658 restored. (Authorised Edition.) Demy 12mo, cloth limp, - - - - - 0 1 4

——— Cloth boards, - - - - - 0 1 6

——— Roan, sprinkled edges, - - - - 0 1 9

——— Roan, gilt edges, - - - - - 0 2 0

——— Superior Edition, printed on superfine paper, extra cloth, bevelled boards, antique, - - - - - - 0 3 6

——— Full calf, lettered, antique, - - - - 0 5 0

——— Without the other Documents. Demy 12mo, stitched, - 0 0 6

Dill (Edward Marcus, A.M., M.D.) The Mystery Solved; or,
Ireland's Miseries; Their Grand Cause and Cure. Foolscap 8vo, cloth, - - - - - - - 0 2 6

——— **The Gathering Storm; or, Britain's Romeward Career: A**
Warning and Appeal to British Protestants. Foolscap 8vo, cloth, - 0 1 0

Family Prayers for Four Weeks. Edited by the Rev. John Hall,
D.D., New York. Extra foolscap 8vo, cloth, - - - 0 2 0

Family Prayers for Working Men (for Two Weeks). By
Ministers of various Evangelical Denominations. Edited, with a Preface, by the Rev. John Hall, D.D., New York. Extra foolscap 8vo, stiffened boards, - - - - - - 0 0 6

——— Limp cloth, - - - - - - 0 0 9

'Fifty-One Hour' Wages Reckoner, The: Consisting of Compu-
tations per Week, and Computations per Hour, for a Working Month. With Supplementary Comparative Table, applicable to Weeks of 48, 54, 57, and 60 Hours respectively. By a Retired Banker. 256 pp., extra foolscap 8vo, cloth, - - - - - 0 2 6

Fleming (Rev. Robert). The Rise and Fall of Papacy. Reprinted
from the Edition of 1701, with a Preface by the late Rev. Thomas Thomson. Extra foolscap 8vo, sewed, - - - 0 1 0

——— Cloth, - - - - - 0 1 6

Forbes (Rev. Robert, A.M.) Digest of Rules and Procedure in
the Inferior Courts of the Free Church of Scotland. With Appendix, embracing a Ministerial Manual, and also containing Forms and Documents. Third Edition, Revised. Extra foolscap 8vo, cloth, - 0 3 6

Habit; with Special Reference to the Formation of a Virtuous
Character. An Address to Students. By Burns Thomson. With a
Recommendatory Note by the late Professor Miller. Second Edition,
Revised. 18mo, - - - - - - £0 0 2

Handbook and Index to the Principal Acts of Assembly of the
Free Church of Scotland—1843-1868. By a Minister of the Free Church
of Scotland. Extra foolscap 8vo, cloth, - - - - 0 2 6

Helps at the Mercy-Seat. Selected from the Scriptures, the Old
Divines, and the Poets. By the Rev. John M. Putnam. Extra fools-
cap 8vo, cloth, - - - - - - 0 2 6
——————— Gilt edges, - - - - - - 0 3 0

Howat (Rev. H. T.) Sabbath Hours: A Series of Meditations on
Gospel Themes. Extra foolscap 8vo, cloth, - - - 0 3 6

Hunter (James J.) Historical Notices of Lady Yester's Church
and Parish, Edinburgh. Compiled from Authentic Sources. Extra
foolscap 8vo, cloth. Printed on Toned Paper, - - - 0 2 6

Hymns for the Use of Sabbath Schools and Bible Classes.
Selected by a Committee of Clergymen. Royal 32mo, sewed, - 0 0 3

Knitting Book of Counterpanes (A). With Diagrams and Direc-
tions. By Mrs George Cupples, Author of 'The Stocking-Knitter's
Manual.' Printed on Toned Paper, with Illuminated Cover. Extra
foolscap 8vo, - - - - - - - 0 0 6

Meikle (Rev. Jas., D.D.) Coming Events. An Inquiry regarding
the Three Prophetical Numbers of the last Chapter of Daniel. Extra
foolscap 8vo, cloth, - - - - - - 0 2 6

Miller (Rev. James N.) Prelacy Tried by the Word of God.
With an Appendix on the Prelatic Argument from Church History.
Foolscap 8vo, limp cloth, - - - - - 0 1 0

Miller (Professor Jas.) Physiology in Harmony with the Bible,
respecting the Value and Right Observance of the Sabbath. Royal
32mo, limp cloth, - - - - - - 0 0 6

Newton (John). Cardiphonia; or, The Utterance of the Heart.
Extra foolscap 8vo, cloth, - - - - - 0 3 0

Ocean Lays. Selected by the Rev. J. Longmuir, LL.D. Illustrated.
Square 16mo, cloth, - - - - - - 0 2 6

Patterson (Alex. S., D.D.) The Redeemer and the Redemption.
Extra foolscap 8vo, cloth, - - - - - 0 2 6

Philip (Rev. John, M.A.) Rays of Light: or, Church-Themes and
Life-Problems. Extra foolscap 8vo, cloth, - - - 0 3 6

Pond (Professor Enoch, D.D.) The Seals Opened; or, The
Apocalypse Explained for Bible Students. Crown 8vo, cloth, - £0 3 6

Rochdale Discourses. By Clergymen connected with the Synod
of the United Presbyterian Church in England. With a Preface by
Professor John Cairns, D.D. Crown 8vo, cloth, - - - 0 5 0

Scots Worthies, The. By John Howie of Lochgoin. A New
Edition. Edited by the Rev. W. H. Carslaw, M.A. Printed on Toned
Paper, with 150 Illustrations on Wood. Demy 8vo, cloth extra, - 0 7 6
——— Calf, antique, red edges, - - - - 0 15 0

Steele (James). A Manual of the Evidences of Christianity.
Chiefly intended for Young Persons. 18mo, cloth, - - 0 1 0

Stocking-Knitter's Manual (The): A Companion for the Work-
Table. By Mrs George Cupples, Author of the 'Knitting Book of
Counterpanes.' Extra foolscap 8vo, Illuminated cover, - - 0 0 6

Sum of Saving Knowledge, The. Extracted from the Westminster
Confession of Faith. For the use of Bible Classes. Super-royal 32mo,
stiffened boards, - - - - - - 0 0 4
——— Cloth limp, - - - - - - 0 0 6

Tasker (Rev. William). The Territorial Visitor's Manual: A
Handbook of Home Mission Work. Small 8vo, cloth, - - 0 2 0

Thompson (Rev. John, A.M.) Life Work of Peter the Apostle.
Extra foolscap 8vo, cloth, - - - - - 0 3 6

Thoughts on Intercessory Prayer. By a Lady.
Royal 32mo, limp cloth, - - - - - 0 0 6

Wallace (Rev. J. A.) Communion Services, according to the
Presbyterian Form. Extra foolscap 8vo, cloth, - - - 0 2 6
——— A Pastor's Legacy.
Extra foolscap 8vo, cloth, - - - - 0 2 6

Watts' (Isaac, D.D.) Divine Songs for Children; with Scripture
Proofs. For the use of Families and Schools. Square 32mo, sewed, - 0 0 2

Wilberforce's Practical View of Christianity. Complete Edition.
Extra foolscap 8vo, cloth, - - - - - 0 2 6

Willison (Rev. John). Sacramental Meditations and Advices for
the use of Communicants. Crown 8vo, cloth, - - - 0 2 6
——— The Afflicted Man's Companion. A New Edition.
Demy 18mo, - - - - - 0 1 6

MUSIC.

The Treasury Hymnal. A Selection of Part Music, in the Ordinary Notation, with Instrumental Accompaniment: the Hymns selected from Dr Bonar's 'Hymns of Faith and Hope.' The Letter-Note Method of Musical Notation is added as a help to young singers. Twenty-four Numbers. (For Contents, see next page.) Super-royal 8vo—each - - - - - - £0 0 1
—— Part I., Nos. 1 to 12, in Printed Wrapper, - - - 0 1 0
—— Part II., Nos. 13 to 24, in Printed Wrapper, - - - 0 1 0
—— The Whole Work complete. Cloth extra, gilt edges, - - 0 3 6

The Children's Harmonist. A Series of Part Songs for the Family and the School-room. Harmonised, on the Letter-Note Method, for Two Voices, with a Bass Accompaniment. By David Colville, Author of 'The Letter-Note Singing Method,' etc. Twelve Numbers. (For Contents, see J. H. & Co.'s separate 'List of Musical Publications.') Super-royal 16mo—each - - - - - 0 0 1
—— The Whole Work complete. Cloth, lettered, - - 0 1 6

Choral Harmony. Edited by David Colville. A Selection of Music, chiefly of an easy character, in Vocal Score, for the use of Choral Societies, Classes, Schools, etc. Upwards of 130 Numbers published. (For Contents, see J. H. & Co.'s separate 'List of Musical Publications.') Royal 8vo—each - - - - - 0 0 1
—— Vol. I. (50 Numbers), cloth boards, - - - - 0 4 0
—— Vol. II. (50 Numbers), cloth boards, - - - - 0 4 0
—— Vols. III. and IV.—*In progress.*

The Letter-Note Singing Method: Elementary Division, in Twenty-three Lessons. By David Colville. Royal 8vo, sewed, - - 0 1 0
—— Cloth, - - - - - - - 0 1 6

The Choral Guide: Being the Exercises contained in the foregoing Work. Two Parts, sold separately—each - - - 0 0 3

A Course of Elementary Practice in Vocal Music. For use in connection with any Method of Solmization. Composed and Arranged by David Colville. Two Parts—each - - - - 0 0 4

A Graduated Course of Elementary Instruction in Singing on the Letter-Note Method (*by means of which any difficulty of learning to Sing from the common Notation can be easily overcome*), in Twenty-six Lessons. By David Colville and George Bentley. Royal 8vo, in Wrapper, - - - - - - 0 1 0
—— Cloth, - - - - - - - 0 1 6

The Pupil's Handbook: Being the Exercises contained in the foregoing Work. For the use of Classes and Schools. Two Parts, sold separately—each - - - - - - 0 0 3

An Elementary Course of Practice in Vocal Music, with numerous Tables, Diagrams, etc., and copious Examples of all the usual Times, Keys, and Changes of Keys. For use in connection with any Method of Solmization. By David Colville. Complete in Two Parts—each - 0 0 4

Colville's Choral School: A Collection of Easy Part Songs, Anthems, etc., in Vocal Score, for the use of Schools and Singing Classes. Arranged progressively, and forming a complete Course of Practice in Vocal Music. In Twenty Parts—each - - - 0 0 4

THE TREASURY HYMNAL:

A Selection of Part Music, in the Ordinary Notation, with Instrumental Accompaniment: the Hymns selected from Dr Bonar's "Hymns of Faith and Hope." The Letter-Note Method of Musical Notation is added as a help to young singers. Twenty-four Numbers. Super-royal 8vo. One Penny each.

1. Forward, - - - - - - *Old Melody.*
   A Bethlehem Hymn, - - - - *Arranged from Mozart.*
2. The Friend, - - - - - *Haydn.*
   Lost but Found, - - - - *Pleyel.*
3. A Little While, - - - *Adapted from Mendelssohn.*
   A Stranger Here, - - - - *Pleyel.*
4. The Blank, - - - - - *Do.*
   The Night and the Morning, - *Adapted from Rode.*
5. The Cloudless, - - - - *Haydn.*
   The Substitute, - - - - *Do.*
6. Thy Way, not Mine, - - - *Altered from Pleyel.*
   Rest Yonder, - - - - *Steibelt.*
7. Ever Near, - - - - - *German Melody.*
   Quis Separabit, - - - - *Beethoven.*
8. All Well, - - - - - *Haydn.*
   Disappointment, - - - - *Do.*
   Child's Prayer, - - - - *Weber.*
9. God's Israel, - - - - *Atterbury.*
   The Elder Brother, - - - *Beethoven.*
   Day Spring, - - - - - *German Melody.*
10. The Night Cometh, - - - *Venetian Melody.*
    How Long, - - - - - *Mendelssohn.*
11. The Two Eras, - - - - *Spohr.*
    The Shepherd's Plain, - - *Whitaker.*
12. Bright Feet of May, - - - *Do.*
    Heaven at Last, - - - - *Clementi.*
13. No Night Descend on Thee, - *Graun.*
    The Voice from Galilee, - - *Kirmair.*
14. The First and the Last, - - *Schubert.*
    Ecce Homo, - - - - - *Mozart.*
15. A Child of Day, - - - - *Spohr.*
    The Shadow of the Cross, - *Haydn.*
16. The Sleep of the Beloved, - *Polish Melody.*
    Strength by the Way, - - *Weber.*
17. The Battle Song of the Church, - *Colville.*
    The Day after Armageddon, - *Hummel.*
18. Sabbath Hymn, - - - - *Dr Miller.*
    Martyr's Hymn, - - - - *Hindostanee Melody*
19. He is Coming, - - - - *Himmel.*
    Live, - - - - - - *Handel.*
20. Summer Gladness, - - - *German Melody.*
    Lines, - - - - - - *Spohr.*
21. Use Me, - - - - - *Anonymous.*
    Smooth Every Wave, - - - *Hering.*
22. Begin with God, - - - *Anonymous.*
    Homewards, - - - - - *Mozart.*
23. The Desert Journey, - - *Hastings.*
    Laus Deo, - - - - - *Bost.*
24. Things Hoped For, - - - *Pleyel.*
    He Liveth Long who Liveth Well, *Beethoven.*

www.ingramcontent.com/pod-product-compliance
Lightning Source LLC
Chambersburg PA
CBHW031747230426
43669CB00007B/519